MOVIE ★ ICONS

PACINO

EDITOR
PAUL DUNCAN

TEXT
F. X. FEENEY

PHOTOS
THE KOBAL COLLECTION

TASCHEN

HONG KONG KÖLN LONDON LOS ANGELES MADRID PARIS TOKYO

CONTENTS

AL PACINO: FORCE OF NATURE

BY F. X. FEENEY

AL PACINO: EINE NATURGEWALT

AL PACINO : FORCE DE LA NATURE

AL PACINO: FORCE OF NATURE

by F. X. Feeney

American cinema, as we've known it since 1972, would be impossible to imagine without Al Pacino. The world at large discovered him that year in his most iconic role—that of Michael Corleone—the resourceful young war hero with a life of infinite possibility ahead of him, who is tragically drawn into his family's criminal enterprise and transformed into the Godfather. The role is Shakespearean in dimension. Michael must become many people to fulfill his destiny. He is by turns a lover, an avenger, a leader, and, finally, often against his will as the *Godfather* films stretch across their epic three parts, a destroyer of all he loves. Pacino is passionately equal to each of these aspects, though the abiding beauty of his performance is that this passion is so fiercely reined in. His Michael Corleone is a magnetic monster of stillness, and silent cunning. He says memorable things, but lets his extraordinary eyes do the real talking.

Pacino extended his range and became a box-office idol. In *Serpico* (1973), he plays Michael's polar opposite—a police detective so resolute in his integrity that he becomes an outcast, shunned and plotted against by the more corrupt policemen with whom he works. In *Dog Day Afternoon* (1975), he radically defies the machismo type of his previous two roles, playing a bisexual bank robber trapped at the center of a comical, nightmarish hostage crisis that he didn't plan, but that he is desperate to master before it buries him.

His subsequent career includes weak films (*Bobby Deerfield*, 1977; *Revolution*, 1985) and lightweight moments where Pacino is merely called upon to echo the explosive menace of his best work (*Ocean's 13*, 2007), yet his choices are always interesting—he finds his way to the great moments, even when the rest of the picture is in chaos. Take *Revolution*. It's a faulty movie, yet near the heart of it Pacino has an extraordinary scene, where he keeps his wounded son alive by talking to him. He tells the boy what they'll do once the American Revolution is behind them, babbling as if spinning a fairy tale. Yet as he does,

STILL FROM 'SCARFACE' (1983)

"It's easy to fool the eye but it's hard to fool the heart."
Al Pacino

we're privileged to see—like a moment of daybreak in the man's eyes—the very idea of "America" being born, a suddenly conscious justification of the revolt this man had, up to now, suffered as a hapless bystander. This moment makes the whole troubled film worthwhile, and is entirely an actor's miracle.

Pacino has kept his private life private. We know he was born poor, knew little of his father growing up, was raised by loving women, and is a father of three but has never married. With the exception of his open conversations with journalist Lawrence Grobel, with whom he formed a bond of instinctive trust, Pacino has studiously avoided publicity. He expressly wishes that we know him, if possible, only through the work.

He's a wonderful devil in *The Devil's Advocate* (1997)—Pacino is never less than wholly energetic and committed to whatever he chooses—but his best and subtlest performances in recent years have been for director Michael Mann, in *Heat* (1995) and *The Insider* (1999). His single most sensational performance is as Tony Montana in *Scarface* (1983), a mobster of a very different stripe from Michael Corleone—a foulmouthed Napoleon Bonaparte climbing with primal energy from the depths of the gutter to the throne of the rubble heap. Pacino finds the humanity in this repugnant man without ever allowing us to romanticize him. This is an exceptional feat, and it rises out of what onetime lover and colleague Jill Clayburgh called Pacino's lack of egotism. Where many actors fall into the trap of wanting to be loved in what they play, Pacino is dedicated first and last to being truthful. As a rival gangster says of Tony Montana, "There is no lying in him." This is equally true of Pacino. Whether the men he plays are good or evil, intimately available or maddeningly remote, he is at all times a man to be trusted. That makes him impossible to ignore. Indeed, it makes him a magnet for our continuing attention—the instant he shows up on-screen, he projects the happy sense that he and we are about to discover something.

AL PACINO: EINE NATURGEWALT

von F. X. Feeney

Man kann sich das amerikanische Kino, wie man es seit 1972 kennt, nicht mehr ohne Al Pacino vorstellen. Die Welt entdeckte ihn in jenem Jahr in der Rolle, die ihn am meisten prägte: als Michael Corleone, ein findiger Kriegsheld, der ein Leben mit allen Möglichkeiten vor sich hat, aber auf tragische Weise in die verbrecherischen Machenschaften seiner Familie hineingezogen wird und sich zum „Paten" wandelt. Die Rolle ist von Shakespeare'scher Dimension. Michael muss in viele Rollen schlüpfen, damit sich sein Schicksal erfüllt. Er ist nacheinander Liebhaber, Rächer, Führer und schließlich – während sich die *Paten*-Trilogie in epischer Breite entwickelt – oft gegen seinen Willen ein Zerstörer all dessen, was ihm lieb ist. Mit Leidenschaft wird Pacino all diesen Facetten seiner Figur gerecht, wenngleich die anhaltende Faszination seines Schauspiels darin liegt, dass er diese Leidenschaft so angespannt im Zaum zu halten versteht. Sein Michael Corleone ist ein anziehendes Ungeheuer, unheimlich ruhig und auf stille Weise durchtrieben. Er gibt denkwürdige Aussprüche von sich, doch das eigentliche Sprechen überlässt er seinen außergewöhnlichen Augen.

Pacino hat sein Spektrum erweitert und ist zu einem Erfolgsgaranten an den Kinokassen geworden. In *Serpico* (1973) spielt er das genaue Gegenteil von Michael: einen Kriminalbeamten, der in seiner Integrität so unbeugsam ist, dass er zum Außenseiter wird, ein Opfer der Ränkespiele seiner korrupten Kollegen, die ihn verachten und mobben. Seine Rolle in *Hundstage* (1975) hat nun gar nichts mehr mit dem Männlichkeitsgehabe seiner beiden vorangegangenen Filmhelden zu tun. Hier spielt er einen bisexuellen Bankräuber, der sich in eine komisch-albtraumhafte Geiselnahme verstrickt, die er nicht geplant hatte und die er nun verzweifelt zu meistern versucht, bevor er von ihr in den Abgrund gerissen wird.

In seiner weiteren Karriere gab es auch schwache Filme (*Bobby Deerfield*, 1977; *Revolution*, 1985) und oberflächliche, in denen Pacino nur die explosive Bedrohlichkeit seiner

PORTRAIT FOR 'SCARECROW' (1973)
Francis (Pacino) is a sweet-spirited drifter on the verge of a nervous breakdown as he seeks to reconnect with his wife and child. / Francis (Pacino), ein gutmütiger Streuner am Rande des Nervenzusammenbruchs, versucht, das Verhältnis zu seiner Frau und seinem Kind zu kitten. / Francis (Pacino) est un brave vagabond au bord de la dépression qui tente de renouer avec son ancienne compagne et son enfant.

„Es ist einfach, das Auge zu täuschen, aber es ist schwer, das Herz zu täuschen."
Al Pacino

Spitzenleistungen zu parodieren hatte (*Ocean's 13*, 2007). Dennoch ist die Wahl seiner Rollen immer interessant – er bahnt sich den Weg zu großartigen Augenblicken, selbst wenn der Rest des Films im Chaos versinkt. Nehmen wir zum Beispiel *Revolution*: ein Film voller Schwächen, aber an zentraler Stelle hat Pacino (Tom) eine außerordentliche Szene, in der er seinen verwundeten Sohn am Leben hält, indem er mit ihm spricht. Tom erzählt dem Jungen, was sie alles machen werden, wenn erst einmal der Kampf um die Unabhängigkeit der Vereinigten Staaten beendet ist; er schwadroniert drauflos, als denke er sich ein Märchen aus. Für den Zuschauer ist es jedoch so, als habe er der Geburt der eigentlichen Idee von „Amerika" zugesehen – eine plötzliche, bewusste Rechtfertigung der Revolte, die Tom bis zu diesem Zeitpunkt lediglich als Unbeteiligter durchlitten hatte. Dieser eine Moment wiegt die Schwächen des ganzen Films auf, ein Wunder, das dieser eine Schauspieler vollbringt.

Pacino hat sein Privatleben privat gehalten. Wir wissen, dass er in armen Verhältnissen zur Welt kam, in seinen jungen Jahren wenig über seinen Vater wusste, von liebenswürdigen Frauen erzogen wurde und drei Kinder hat, aber nie verheiratet war. Abgesehen von seinen offenen Gesprächen mit dem Journalisten Lawrence Grobel, dem er instinktiv vertraute, hat Pacino geflissentlich jegliche Publicity gemieden. Er wünscht ausdrücklich, dass wir ihn, wenn möglich, ausschließlich durch seine Arbeit kennen.

Er ist ein wunderbarer Teufel in *Im Auftrag des Teufels* (1997) – stets mit vollem Einsatz bei der Sache, wenn er sich einmal für eine Rolle entschieden hat –, aber seine besten und subtilsten Leistungen in den letzten Jahren entstanden unter der Regie von Michael Mann in *Heat* (1995) und *Insider* (1999). Seine sensationellste Leistung überhaupt war die Rolle des Tony Montana in *Scarface* (1983), eines Mafioso von gänzlich anderem Zuschnitt als Michael Corleone: eine Art „Gossen-Napoleon", der mit urwüchsiger Energie aus den gesellschaftlichen Niederungen zum Thron des Müllbergs aufsteigt. Pacino findet die menschliche Seite dieses widerwärtigen Zeitgenossen, ohne ihn romantisch zu verklären. Das ist eine außerordentliche Leistung, die weit über das hinausgeht, was seine Kollegin und Exgeliebte Jill Clayburgh als Pacinos Mangel an Selbstgefälligkeit bezeichnete. Wo viele Schauspieler in die Falle tappen, in ihrer Rolle geliebt werden zu wollen, geht es Pacino in allererster Linie darum, glaubwürdig zu sein. „In ihm ist nichts Verlogenes", sagt ein rivalisierender Gangster über Tony Montana, und das trifft gleichermaßen auf Pacino zu. Ob er einen guten oder bösen Typen spielt, einen leicht zugänglichen oder wahnsinnig fernen: Er ist immer ein Mensch, dem man vertrauen kann. Es ist unmöglich, ihn zu ignorieren. Tatsächlich zieht er auf diese Weise ständig unsere Aufmerksamkeit auf sich – sobald er auf der Leinwand auftaucht, vermittelt er das freudige Gefühl, dass er und wir gleich im Begriff sind, etwas zu entdecken.

PORTRAIT FOR 'CRUISING' (1980)

As macho detective Steve Burns, gazing into the abyss under his once placid male identity as he works undercover protecting homosexuals. / Für den Macho Steve Burns, der seine Identität als Mann bisher nie in Zweifel zog, tun sich Abgründe auf, als der Kripobeamte verdeckt ermittelt, um Homosexuelle zu beschützen. / Steve Burns, policier macho chargé d'enquêter sur des meurtres d'homosexuels, découvre des zones d'ombre sous son identité masculine bien affirmée.

AL PACINO: FORCE DE LA NATURE

F. X. Feeney

Le cinéma américain tel que nous le connaissons depuis le début des années 1970 serait impossible à imaginer sans Al Pacino. C'est en effet en 1972 que le monde entier découvre cet acteur dans son rôle le plus légendaire, celui de Michael Corleone dans *Le Parrain*. Un jeune héros de guerre à l'avenir prometteur qui se retrouve tragiquement impliqué dans les affaires criminelles de sa famille et devient un parrain de la mafia. Personnage d'envergure shakespearienne, Michael Corleone doit devenir un homme aux multiples facettes pour accomplir son destin. Tour à tour amant, vengeur, chef de gang et enfin, au fil des trois volets de cette épopée, ange exterminateur détruisant à contrecœur tous ceux qu'il aime. Al Pacino incarne avec passion et maestria chacune de ces facettes, même si la beauté immuable de son interprétation réside dans l'acharnement avec lequel il réprime cette passion. Entre ses mains, Michael Corleone devient un monstre d'imperturbabilité et de fourberie glacée. S'il prononce quelques paroles mémorables, c'est son extraordinaire regard qui en dit le plus long.

Al Pacino élargit ensuite son répertoire et devient une idole du box-office. Dans *Serpico* (1973), il incarne l'opposé absolu de Michael Corleone, un policier si déterminé dans son intégrité qu'il se retrouve marginalisé, victime de l'ostracisme et des complots de ses collègues corrompus. Dans *Un après-midi de chien* (1975), il dément radicalement le machisme de ses deux rôles précédents en interprétant un braqueur de banque bisexuel coincé dans l'engrenage d'une prise d'otages imprévue, situation à la fois comique et cauchemardesque qu'il tente désespérément de maîtriser avant d'y être englouti.

Bien que la suite de sa carrière contienne quelques films plus médiocres (*Bobby Deerfield*, 1977 ; *Révolution*, 1985) et certaines œuvres légères où sa présence sert uniquement à évoquer la violence explosive de ses meilleures prestations (*Ocean's 13*, 2007), ses

STILL FROM 'HEAT' (1995)
L.A. cop Vincent Hanna, one of the best-known characters of Pacino's career, is, first and last, a relentless "hunter." / Der Cop Vincent Hanna aus L.A., eine der bekanntesten Figuren in Pacinos Karriere, ist vor allem ein unerbittlicher „Jäger". / Le policier Vincent Hanna, l'un des personnages les plus célèbres de la carrière d'Al Pacino, est avant tout un impitoyable « chasseur ».

« Il est facile de tromper l'œil,
mais il est plus difficile de tromper le cœur. »
Al Pacino

choix demeurent toujours intéressants. Même lorsque le reste du film sombre dans le chaos, l'acteur parvient à en sublimer les meilleurs moments. Prenons l'exemple de *Révolution*, œuvre certes imparfaite, mais dans laquelle Al Pacino interprète une scène extraordinaire. Afin de maintenir en vie son fils blessé, il lui raconte ce qu'ils feront une fois la Révolution américaine achevée, débitant son histoire à la manière d'un conte de fées. Mais durant son récit, le spectateur assiste émerveillé – comme s'il voyait poindre l'aube dans son regard – à la naissance de l'idée même d'«Amérique», soudaine justification de la révolte que cet homme a jusque-là subie en spectateur impuissant. Véritable miracle de la part de l'acteur, cette scène suffit à conférer au film un réel intérêt.

Al Pacino a su préserver sa vie privée. On sait qu'il est né dans un milieu pauvre, n'a guère connu son père, a été élevé avec amour dans un entourage féminin, a donné le jour à trois enfants mais ne s'est jamais marié. À l'exception de ses confidences au journaliste Lawrence Grobel, auquel il a voué une confiance instinctive, Al Pacino a toujours savamment évité le feu des médias. Son vœu le plus cher est de n'être connu, si possible, que par le biais de ses œuvres.

S'il campe un savoureux Satan dans *L'Associé du diable* (1997) – car il est incapable de se donner à moins de 100 % aux rôles qu'il choisit –, c'est au réalisateur Michael Mann qu'il a récemment réservé ses prestations les plus subtiles, aussi bien dans *Heat* (1995) que dans *Révélations* (1999). Son interprétation la plus sensationnelle demeure toutefois celle de Tony Montana dans *Scarface* (1983), un mafieux d'un tout autre acabit que Michael Corleone, sorte de Bonaparte mal embouché gravissant avec une énergie incontrôlable les échelons qui le mènent des profondeurs du caniveau au sommet du tas d'ordures. Al Pacino révèle l'humanité de cet être répugnant sans jamais sombrer dans l'idéalisation. Un véritable tour de maître qui s'explique par ce que son ancienne maîtresse et partenaire Jill Clayburgh appelle l'«absence totale d'égocentrisme» d'Al Pacino. Alors que tant d'acteurs tombent dans le piège de vouloir être aimés à travers leurs personnages, Al Pacino n'a qu'une idée en tête : la vérité. Comme le dit un rival de Tony Montana, «il n'y a pas de mensonge en lui». C'est également le cas d'Al Pacino. Que les personnages qu'il incarne soient bons ou mauvais, intimement proches ou monstrueusement distants, c'est un homme à qui l'on peut se fier. Et c'est pourquoi il exerce une telle attraction. Sans cesse à l'affût de découvertes qu'il semble prêt à nous faire partager dès l'instant où il apparaît à l'écran, Al Pacino attire notre attention aussi irrésistiblement qu'un aimant.

PAGE 22

PORTRAIT FOR
'THE PANIC IN NEEDLE PARK' (1971)
After years of attention-getting work on the New York stage, Pacino made his first mark here, playing the drug addict Bobby. / Nach Jahren viel beachteter Auftritte auf New Yorker Bühnen, profilierte sich Pacino in der Rolle des drogenabhängigen Bobby erstmals auch auf der Leinwand. / Après s'être produit pendant des années sur les scènes new-yorkaises, Al Pacino se fait un nom en interprétant un toxicomane nommé Bobby.

PORTRAIT FOR
'THE GODFATHER: PART II' (1974)
As loyal son and haunted crime boss Michael Corleone, the single most iconic figure brought to life by Al Pacino. / Michael Corleone, loyaler Sohn und von Heimsuchungen geplagter Mafiaboss, ist unter all seinen Rollen die Kultfigur schlechthin, die Al Pacino mit Leben erfüllte. / Michael Corleone, fils dévoué et parrain tourmenté, est le personnage le plus emblématique de la carrière d'Al Pacino.

2

VISUAL FILMOGRAPHY

FILMOGRAFIE IN BILDERN

FILMOGRAPHIE EN IMAGES

**STILL FROM
'THE PANIC IN NEEDLE PARK' (1971)**
Kitty Winn (left) had won kudos as Saint Joan, onstage, and won the award for best actress at Cannes for her performance here. / Kitty Winn (links) war auf der Bühne für ihre Darstellung der heiligen Johanna von Orléans gefeiert worden und wurde nun für diese Rolle bei den Filmfestspielen in Cannes als beste Schauspielerin ausgezeichnet. / Kitty Winn (à gauche), qui a été saluée pour son interprétation de Sainte Jeanne au théâtre, remporte le prix d'interprétation féminine à Cannes pour ce rôle.

**STILL FROM
'THE PANIC IN NEEDLE PARK' (1971)**
"Romeo and Juliet on junk" is how screenwriters John Gregory Dunne and Joan Didion pitched this adaptation of James Mills's book. / Als „Romeo und Julia auf Drogen" verkauften die Drehbuchautoren John Gregory Dunne und Joan Didion ihre Adaption des Buchs von James Mills. / « Roméo et Juliette sous héroïne », telle est la formule employée par les scénaristes John Gregory Dunne et Joan Didion pour résumer cette adaptation du roman de James Mills.

**STILL FROM
'THE PANIC IN NEEDLE PARK' (1971)**
The heroin-addicted denizens of "Needle Park," with
Pacino enthroned dead center, Kitty Winn at his left. /
Die heroinsüchtigen Bewohner des "Needle Park" mit
Pacino, der genau in ihrer Mitte thront, und Kitty Winn
zu seiner Linken. / Les héroïnomanes de « Needle
Park » : Pacino trône au centre, avec Kitty Winn à
sa gauche.

*"I learned a lot of my craft from children.
Kids really turn me on—they are the most
uninhibited audience of all."*
Al Pacino

*„Ich habe einen Großteil meines Handwerks von
Kindern gelernt. Kinder begeistern mich - sie sind
die ungehemmtesten Zuschauer von allen."*
Al Pacino

*« Professionnellement, j'ai beaucoup appris de
mes enfants. Les gosses me donnent des ailes,
c'est le public le plus désinhibé qui soit. »*
Al Pacino

**STILL FROM
'THE PANIC IN NEEDLE PARK' (1971)**
The film at times affects a "handheld" vérité style, and
Pacino was so convincing it won him a screen test for
The Godfather. / Manchmal bediente sich der Film in
Form der Handkamera eines Stilmittels des cinéma
vérité, und Pacino spielte so überzeugend, dass er zu
einer Kameraprobe für den *Paten* eingeladen wurde. /
Dans ce film adoptant par moments un style « caméra
à l'épaule », la prestation de Pacino est si convaincante
qu'il décroche un bout d'essai pour *Le Parrain*.

PORTRAIT FOR 'THE GODFATHER' (1972)
With older brother Sonny (James Caan), father Don
Vito Corleone (Marlon Brando), and fragile brother
Fredo (John Cazale). / Mit seinem älteren Bruder Sonny
(James Caan), seinem Vater Don Vito Corleone (Marlon
Brando) und seinem schwächlichen Bruder Fredo (John
Cazale). / Avec son frère aîné Sonny (James Caan), son
père Don Vito Corleone (Marlon Brando) et son frère
cadet, le fragile Fredo (John Cazale).

PORTRAIT FOR 'THE GODFATHER' (1972)
Michael Corleone, war hero, with ambitions outside the
Mob, suffers a disfiguring punch while defending his
father's life. / Michael Corleone, ein Kriegsheld, der sich
Ziele außerhalb der Mafia gesteckt hat, wird von einem
Schlag ins Gesicht entstellt, als er das Leben seines
Vaters verteidigt. / Héros de guerre nourrissant des
ambitions à l'extérieur de la Mafia, Michael Corleone
est défiguré par un coup de poing en sauvant la vie
de son père.

STILL FROM 'THE GODFATHER' (1972)
A baptism of blood: Michael commits his first crime, a killing in revenge for the attempt on his father's life. / Eine Blutstaufe: Michael begeht sein erstes Verbrechen – einen Mord aus Rache für den Anschlag auf das Leben seines Vaters. / Baptême du sang: Michael commet son premier meurtre en représailles contre la tentative d'assassinat de son père.

"My father made him an offer he couldn't refuse."
Michael Corleone, *The Godfather* **(1972)**

„Mein Vater hat ihm ein Angebot gemacht, das er nicht ablehnen konnte."
Michael Corleone, *Der Pate* **(1972)**

« Mon père lui a fait une offre qu'il ne pouvait refuser. »
Michael Corleone, *Le Parrain* **(1972)**

STILL FROM 'THE GODFATHER' (1972)
Killing the corrupt Irish cop who punched him (Sterling
Hayden, left) and Sollozzo the Turk (Al Lettieri, dying,
center). / Michael erschießt den korrupten irischen
Polizisten, der ihn geschlagen hatte (Sterling Hayden,
links), und Sollozzo, den ‚Türken' (Al Lettieri, sterbend,
Mitte). / Michael abat le policier corrompu qui l'a
frappé (Sterling Hayden, à gauche) et Sollozzo le Turc
(Al Lettieri, mourant, au centre).

"That's my family, Kay, that's not me."
Michael Corleone, *The Godfather* (1972)

„Das ist meine Familie, Kay, das bin nicht ich."
Michael Corleone, *Der Pate* (1972)

« C'est ma famille, Kay, ce n'est pas moi. »
Michael Corleone, *Le Parrain* (1972)

STILL FROM 'THE GODFATHER' (1972)
Michael is obliged to lie low for a time in Sicily, where he recovers his roots and strengthens his ties to the Corleone crime family. / Michael muss sich eine Zeit lang in Sizilien verstecken, wo er seine Wurzeln wiederentdeckt und seine Bande zum Mafiaclan der Corleones stärkt. / Contraint de se faire oublier quelque temps en Sicile, Michael renoue avec ses racines et resserre ses liens avec le clan Corleone.

STILL FROM 'THE GODFATHER' (1972)
For a brief time, Michael Corleone marries a local
beauty, Apollonia (Simonetta Stefanelli, in bridal gown),
but this union is doomed. / Michael Corleone ist kurze
Zeit mit der Dorfschönheit Apollonia (Simonetta
Stefanelli, im Brautkleid) verheiratet, doch diese Ehe
steht unter einem schlechten Stern. / Michael Corleone
épouse une beauté des environs, Apollonia (Simonetta
Stefanelli, en robe de mariée), mais leur union est vouée
à un sort tragique.

STILL FROM 'THE GODFATHER' (1972)
Assuming the mantle of heir apparent to "the don of dons," Pacino was in his element opposite Brando, "the actor of actors." / In seiner Rolle des Thronfolgers für den „Don der Dons" war Pacino an der Seite Brandos, des „Schauspielers der Schauspieler", in seinem Element. / Endossant le rôle d'héritier présomptif du « roi des parrains », Al Pacino est dans son élément face à Brando, « le roi des acteurs ».

STILL FROM 'THE GODFATHER' (1972)
"I wanted better things for you." Don Corleone (Marlon Brando) sees with regret the hard life into which he has drawn his gifted son. / „Ich wollte Besseres für dich." Don Corleone (Marlon Brando) erkennt reumütig, in welch unerbittliches Leben er seinen begabten Sohn hineingezogen hat. / Constatant avec regret la rude existence dans laquelle il a entraîné son fils, Don Corleone (Marlon Brando) lui confie qu'il avait « espéré autre chose pour lui ».

"I think he projects such power because of his total lack of egocentricity. A lot of actors want to be sexy, cute, adorable [...] Do anything to win an audience to their side [...] Cater to every cheap, trendy, obvious appeal that will make them laugh. Al couldn't care less. He's too honest, and he loves the characters he plays too deeply to go in for that sort of thing. That's why he can turn acting into poetry."

Jill Clayburgh

„Ich denke, er strahlt eine solche Kraft aus, weil er in keiner Weise selbstgefällig ist. Viele Schauspieler möchten sexy, hübsch, liebenswert sein [...] tun alles, um das Publikum auf ihre Seite zu ziehen [...] bedienen sich jedes billigen, modischen, offensichtlichen Tricks, um es zum Lachen zu bringen. Al ist das völlig egal. Er ist zu aufrichtig, und er mag die Figuren, die er spielt, zu sehr, um sich auf so etwas einzulassen. Deshalb kann er Schauspielerei zur Poesie werden lassen."

Jill Clayburgh

«S'il dégage une telle puissance, c'est à cause de son absence totale d'égocentrisme. Beaucoup d'acteurs veulent être sexy, craquants, adorables [...] sont prêts à tout pour mettre le public de leur côté [...] exploitent n'importe quel ressort facile ou à la mode pour faire rire. Al s'en moque éperdument. Il est trop honnête et il aime trop profondément les personnages qu'il joue pour s'adonner à ce genre de choses. C'est ce qui confère à son jeu une sorte de poésie.»

Jill Clayburgh

PORTRAIT FOR 'THE GODFATHER' (1972)
Youthful beauty, but hardened from the inside by what he must become—surely the defining role of Al Pacino's early career. / Jugendliche Schönheit, jedoch von innen heraus gehärtet durch das, was ihm bestimmt ist - zweifelsohne die prägende Rolle in der frühen Karriere Al Pacinos. / Une beauté juvénile endurcie par le destin qui l'attend : le rôle le plus marquant des débuts d'Al Pacino.

STILL FROM 'SCARECROW' (1973)
Max (Gene Hackman), just out of San Quentin Prison, is a man of few words who is also hitching east to make a new start in life. / Max (Gene Hackman), gerade aus dem Gefängnis von San Quentin entlassen, ist ein Mann weniger Worte, der ebenfalls nach Osten unterwegs ist, um im Leben einen Neuanfang zu wagen. / Tout droit sorti de la prison de San Quentin, Max (Gene Hackman) est un homme taciturne qui se rend également en stop vers la côte Est pour démarrer une nouvelle vie.

PORTRAIT FOR 'SCARECROW' (1973)
Francis (Pacino), fresh out of the Navy, hitchhikes across the United States to attempt a reunion with the wife and child he abandoned. / Francis (Pacino), frisch aus der Marine entlassen, schlägt sich per Anhalter quer durch die USA, um wieder zu seiner Frau und seinem Sohn zurückzufinden, die er im Stich gelassen hatte. / Frais émoulu de la Marine, Francis (Pacino) traverse les États-Unis en stop pour tenter de retrouver la compagne et l'enfant qu'il a abandonnés.

STILL FROM 'SCARECROW' (1973)
As the two men travel across America, some of Francis's gentleness rubs off on hard-nosed Max, making him a better person. / Während die beiden gemeinsam durch die USA trampen, färbt Francis' Sanftmut ein wenig auf den abgebrühten Max ab und macht aus ihm einen besseren Menschen. / Pendant leur traversée de l'Amérique, la gentillesse de Francis finit par déteindre sur Max, un dur à cuire qui s'adoucit peu à peu.

PAGES 40/41
STILL FROM 'SCARECROW' (1973)
Francis, who loves children, is first and last a child himself. While he is not quite capable of fatherly responsibility, his is a big breaking heart. / Der kinderliebe Francis ist selbst noch ein Kind geblieben. Wenngleich er nicht ganz in der Lage ist, väterliche Verantwortung zu übernehmen, hat er doch ein großes und leicht zerbrechliches Herz. / Si Francis adore les enfants, c'est qu'il en est un lui-même. Peu apte à assumer ses responsabilités parentales, c'est un être fragile au grand cœur.

STILL FROM 'SCARECROW' (1973)
Told his baby boy died, Francis has a catastrophic
mental breakdown while playing with children in a
fountain. / Als er erfährt, dass sein Baby gestorben
ist, erleidet Francis einen furchtbaren
Nervenzusammenbruch, während er in einem Brunnen
mit Kindern spielt. / Après avoir appris la mort de son
fils, Francis s'effondre psychologiquement en jouant
avec des enfants dans une fontaine.

ON THE SET OF 'SERPICO' (1973)
Director Sidney Lumet in close conference with Pacino. The floppy hat is both a disguise and an expression of real eccentricity. / Regisseur Sidney Lumet berät sich mit Pacino. Der Schlapphut ist einerseits Verkleidung und andererseits Ausdruck echter Exzentrizität. / Le réalisateur Sidney Lumet en grande conversation avec Al Pacino, dont le chapeau mou est à la fois un déguisement et l'expression d'une réelle excentricité.

PORTRAIT FOR 'SERPICO' (1973)
The other iconic role of Pacino's early career is Frank Serpico, the real-life New York detective who fought against police corruption. / Die andere prägende Rolle in Pacinos früher Karriere ist Frank Serpico, der tatsächlich existierende New Yorker Kripobeamte, der gegen Korruption in den eigenen Reihen kämpfte. / L'autre rôle emblématique des débuts d'Al Pacino est celui de Serpico, l'histoire vraie d'un policier new-yorkais parti en croisade contre la corruption de la police.

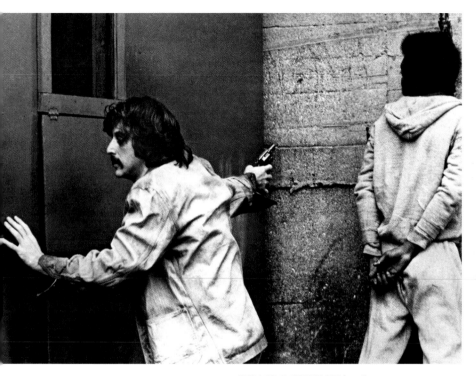

STILL FROM 'SERPICO' (1973)
He is such an effective undercover cop that he has to keep checking over his shoulder to make sure his colleagues don't shoot him. / Zur überzeugenden Darstellung des verdeckten Ermittlers gehörte, dass er sich ständig umdrehen musste, um nicht von den eigenen Kollegen erschossen zu werden. / Son camouflage est si efficace qu'il doit sans cesse regarder par-dessus son épaule pour s'assurer que ses collègues ne lui tirent pas dessus.

STILL FROM 'SERPICO' (1973)
Pacino's sexy, heavy-lidded stare allows us to recognize Frank Serpico under the depths of any disguise. / Pacinos erotisierender Schlafzimmerblick ist immer zu erkennen, mag sich Frank Serpico noch so sehr verkleiden. / Avec ses paupières lourdes et son regard séduisant, Al Pacino alias Frank Serpico est reconnaissable sous n'importe quel déguisement.

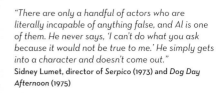

"There are only a handful of actors who are literally incapable of anything false, and Al is one of them. He never says, 'I can't do what you ask because it would not be true to me.' He simply gets into a character and doesn't come out."
Sidney Lumet, director of Serpico (1973) and Dog Day Afternoon (1975)

„Es gibt nur eine Handvoll Schauspieler, die buchstäblich der Heuchelei unfähig sind, und Al ist einer von ihnen. Er sagt nie: ‚Ich kann das, was Sie von mir verlangen, nicht tun, weil es nicht meinem Charakter entspricht.' Er schlüpft einfach in die Figur hinein und kommt nicht wieder heraus."
Sidney Lumet, Regisseur von Serpico (1973) und Hundstage (1975)

« Il n'existe qu'une poignée d'acteurs qui sont absolument incapables de sonner faux, et Al en fait partie. Il ne dit jamais : "Je ne peux pas faire ce que tu me demandes car ça ne sonnerait pas vrai." Il se contente d'entrer dans le personnage et de ne plus en ressortir. »
Sidney Lumet, réalisateur de Serpico (1973) et d'Un après-midi de chien (1975)

STILL FROM 'SERPICO' (1973)
An idealist, meditating sadly on the corrupt workings of the world. / Ein Idealist, der traurig über die korrupten Machenschaften der Welt sinniert. / Un idéaliste en train de méditer tristement sur le fonctionnement corrompu du monde.

STILL FROM 'THE GODFATHER: PART II' (1974)
Pacino, opposite a different sort of icon—great acting
teacher Lee Strasberg in his first film role, as mobster
Hyman Roth. / Pacino neben einer Kultfigur anderer
Art: der großartige Schauspiellehrer Lee Strasberg in
seiner ersten Filmrolle als jüdischer Gangsterboss
Hyman Roth. / Al Pacino aux côtés d'un autre mythe :
le grand professeur d'art dramatique Lee Strasberg
dans son premier rôle au cinéma, celui du mafioso
Hyman Roth.

**PORTRAIT FOR
'THE GODFATHER: PART II' (1974)**
Michael Corleone, literally the second godfather of the
trilogy—older, wiser, bearing a more cruel burden within
himself. / Michael Corleone ist buchstäblich der zweite
Pate in der Trilogie - älter und weiser geworden, trägt er
nun auch eine grausame Last auf seinen Schultern. /
Michael Corleone, le deuxième parrain de la trilogie :
plus vieux, plus sage, accablé d'un plus cruel fardeau
intérieur.

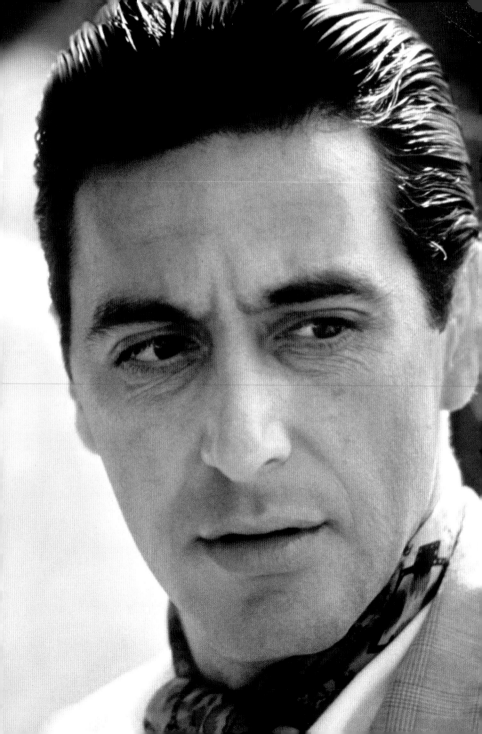

"If anything in this life is certain, if history has taught us anything, it is that you can kill anyone."
Michael Corleone, *The Godfather: Part II* (1974)

„*Wenn es in diesem Leben irgendetwas gibt, das sicher ist, wenn uns die Geschichte irgendetwas gelehrt hat, dann ist es, dass man jeden umbringen kann.*"
Michael Corleone, *Der Pate: Teil 2* (1974)

« *S'il y a une chose qui est sûre dans la vie, s'il y a une chose que l'histoire nous a apprise, c'est qu'on peut tuer n'importe qui.* »
Michael Corleone, *Le Parrain, 2ᵉ partie* (1974)

PAGES 52/53
STILL FROM
'THE GODFATHER: PART II' (1974)
Throughout the film, Pacino must internalize all his intense reactions, which is why he eventually had a breakdown during the shoot. / Während des gesamten Films musste Pacino seine heftigen Reaktionen verinnerlichen, was schließlich auch dazu führte, dass er während der Dreharbeiten zusammenbrach. / Contraint d'intérioriser ses intenses réactions tout au long du film, Al Pacino finit par sombrer dans la dépression durant le tournage.

RIGHT/RECHTS/CI-CONTRE
STILL FROM
'THE GODFATHER: PART II' (1974)
"You broke my heart, Fredo." Yet another downward twist in the saga of Michael Corleone—betrayed by his most gentle brother. / „Du hast mir das Herz gebrochen, Fredo." Eine weitere Wendung zum Schlimmeren in der Saga um Michael Corleone: Er wird von seinem sanftmütigsten Bruder verraten. / « Tu m'as brisé le cœur, Fredo. » Trahi par son frère cadet, Michael Corleone encaisse encore un mauvais coup du sort.

PAGES 56/57
STILL FROM
'THE GODFATHER: PART II' (1974)
Triumphant over his enemies (among them his wife and brother), master of all he surveys—but as dark and alone as Lucifer. / Triumphator über all seine Feinde (darunter seine Ehefrau und sein Bruder), Herrscher über sein Reich – und doch finster und einsam wie Luzifer. / Triomphant de ses ennemis (dont sa femme et son frère) et régnant en maître, Michael semble aussi sombre et solitaire que Lucifer.

STILL FROM 'DOG DAY AFTERNOON' (1975)
One of Pacino's most memorable roles is Sonny
Wortzik, the charming bank robber who (hard as he
tries) is never clever enough. / Eine der denkwürdigsten
Rollen, die Pacino spielte, ist die des Sonny Wortzik,
eines charmanten Bankräubers, der – sosehr er sich
auch bemüht – seiner Sache nie gewachsen ist. / L'un
des rôles les plus mémorables d'Al Pacino est celui de
Sonny Wortzik, charmant braqueur de banque qui ne
parvient pas à déjouer la police.

STILL FROM 'DOG DAY AFTERNOON' (1975)
Sonny's partner, Sal (John Cazale), is ignorant—he thinks
"Montana" is a country outside the United States—and a
bit trigger-happy. / Sonnys Partner Sal (John Cazale) ist
nicht nur ungebildet – er hält Montana für ein Land
außerhalb der USA –, sondern hat auch einen nervösen
Finger am Abzug. / Sal (John Cazale), le complice de
Sonny, est un jeune homme inculte qui prend le
Montana pour un pays étranger et a la gâchette un
peu trop facile.

"ATTICA! ATTICA! ATTICA! ATTICA! ATTICA! ATTICA! ATTICA! ATTICA! ATTICA! ATTICA!"
Sonny Wortzik, *Dog Day Afternoon* (1975)

„ATTICA! ATTICA! ATTICA! ATTICA! ATTICA! ATTICA! ATTICA! ATTICA! ATTICA! ATTICA!"
Sonny Wortzik, *Hundstage* (1975)

« ATTICA ! ATTICA ! ATTICA ! ATTICA ! ATTICA ! ATTICA ! ATTICA ! ATTICA ! ATTICA ! ATTICA ! »
Sonny Wortzik, *Un après-midi de chien* (1975)

STILL FROM 'DOG DAY AFTERNOON' (1975)

One example of Sonny's spontaneity and boldness as a criminal is that he rouses a crowd of onlookers to protest police brutality at Attica Prison. / Sonnys Verwegenheit und Spontaneität zeigen sich unter anderem, als er die Menge der Schaulustigen vor der Bank aufruft, gegen die Brutalität der Aufseher im Gefängnis von Attica zu protestieren. / La scène où il incite une foule de spectateurs à protester contre la brutalité policière à la prison d'Attica illustre bien la spontanéité et l'audace de Sonny.

STILL FROM 'DOG DAY AFTERNOON' (1975)
Sonny doesn't want to hurt anyone. He is even
sympathetic for being at such passionate odds with the
circumstances of his own life. / Sonny möchte
niemandem wehtun. Er wirkt sogar sympathisch, weil er
mit Leidenschaft bei der Sache ist, obwohl er nicht
einmal sein eigenes Leben im Griff hat. / Sonny ne veut
de mal à personne et se montre si passionnément
décalé par rapport à son existence qu'il en devient
sympathique.

"Who speaks of triumph? Endurance is everything!"
Al Pacino

„Wer redet von Triumph? Durchhalten ist alles!"
Al Pacino

*« Qui parle de triomphe ? Tout est question
d'endurance ! »*
Al Pacino

STILL FROM 'DOG DAY AFTERNOON' (1975)
Much as Sonny appears to be in command of the
situation, something in him knows better. Pacino subtly
makes that visible to us. / Obwohl Sonny nach außen
wirkt, als sei er Herr der Lage, weiß er es tief in seinem
Inneren besser, was Pacino auf subtile Weise dem
Zuschauer zu verstehen gibt. / Bien que Sonny
semble maîtriser la situation, Pacino nous fait
imperceptiblement sentir le doute qui s'insinue en lui.

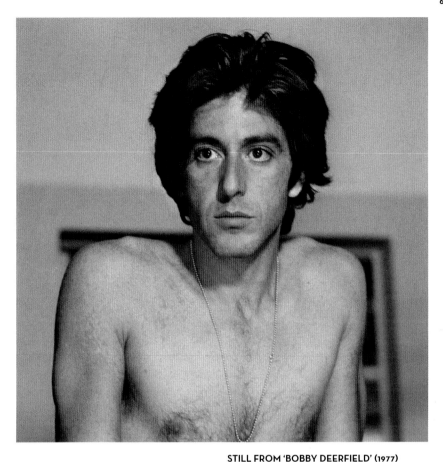

STILL FROM 'BOBBY DEERFIELD' (1977)
This ambitious study of fame and its isolations proved to be one of the few critical and commercial duds of Pacino's career. / Diese ehrgeizige Studie über den Ruhm und die damit einhergehende Vereinsamung gehört zu den wenigen Filmen in Pacinos Karriere, die sowohl bei der Kritik als auch beim Publikum durchfielen. / Cette réflexion ambitieuse sur la célébrité et l'isolement qu'elle provoque est l'un des rares échecs critiques et commerciaux de la carrière d'Al Pacino.

ON THE SET OF 'BOBBY DEERFIELD' (1977)
Pacino later reflected, of director Sydney Pollack (right): "Maybe we would've been better off if I'd listened to him more." / Pacino meinte später einmal über Regisseur Sydney Pollack (rechts): „Vielleicht wäre es besser für uns gewesen, wenn ich öfter mal auf ihn gehört hätte." / Al Pacino confiera plus tard au sujet de Sydney Pollack (à droite) : « J'aurais peut-être mieux fait de l'écouter un peu plus. »

STILL FROM 'BOBBY DEERFIELD' (1977)
With Marthe Keller. For Pacino this film was "about breaking [through] depression, self-absorption; opening like a flower." / Mit Marthe Keller. Für Pacino ging es in diesem Film darum, „Versenkung in sich selbst, Depression zu überwinden, sich wie eine Blume zu öffnen". / Avec Marthe Keller. Pour Pacino, ce film montre comment « percer la dépression et l'égocentrisme, s'ouvrir comme une fleur ».

STILL FROM 'BOBBY DEERFIELD' (1977)
Mortality is the theme that Pollack sought to confront, and that attracted Pacino—the actions a man will take to live more deeply. / Pollack versuchte, die Sterblichkeit zu thematisieren, und das reizte Pacino: was ein Mann alles unternimmt, um intensiver zu leben. / Le thème que Pollack a voulu aborder et qui a attiré Pacino est la mortalité, ce qu'un homme est prêt à faire pour vivre plus intensément.

STILL FROM '... AND JUSTICE FOR ALL' (1979)
Once again Pacino acts opposite his old acting teacher
Lee Strasberg, here playing his grandfather. / Noch
einmal spielt Pacino an der Seite seines alten
Schauspiellehrers Lee Strasberg, der hier seinen
Großvater spielt. / Al Pacino se retrouve à nouveau
aux côtés de son ancien professeur Lee Strasberg,
qui incarne ici son grand-père.

STILL FROM '... AND JUSTICE FOR ALL' (1979)
As a flamboyant trial lawyer, drawing upon the same
buoyant energies that propelled his bank robber in *Dog
Day Afternoon*. / Als großspuriger Strafverteidiger legt
Pacino die gleiche Lebhaftigkeit an den Tag, die schon
seinem Bankräuber in *Hundstage* Antrieb gab. / Dans le
rôle d'un avocat impétueux qui se nourrit de la même
énergie vitale que le personnage du braqueur de
banque dans *Un après-midi de chien*.

"You're out of order! You're out of order!
The whole trial is out of order!"
Arthur Kirkland, ... And Justice for All (1979)

„Sie verstoßen gegen die Verfahrensregeln!
Sie verstoßen gegen die Verfahrensregeln!
Das ganze Verfahren ist verfahren!"
Arthur Kirkland, ... und Gerechtigkeit für alle (1979)

« Vous êtes irrecevable ! Vous êtes irrecevable !
L'ensemble de ce procès est irrecevable ! »
Arthur Kirkland, Justice pour tous (1979)

STILL FROM '... AND JUSTICE FOR ALL' (1979)
Pacino is wonderfully equal to the high comedy and
drama of this role, even though the film's busy action at
times begs disbelief. / Pacino wird auf wunderbare
Weise sowohl der Komik als auch der Dramatik dieser
Rolle gerecht, wenngleich die hektische Handlung des
Films dessen Glaubwürdigkeit bisweilen infrage stellt. /
Al Pacino est parfaitement à l'aise dans les aspects
comiques et dramatiques de ce rôle, même si les scènes
d'action ne sont pas toujours crédibles.

STILL FROM 'CRUISING' (1980)
A macho undercover cop must pretend to be homosexual to trap a serial killer—but he is seduced by this once alien way of life. / Ein verdeckt ermittelnder Macho gibt sich als Homosexueller aus, um einen Serienmörder zu stellen - doch diese Lebensweise, die ihm zuvor völlig fremd war, übt plötzlich auch einen Reiz auf ihn aus. / Policier macho contraint de se faire passer pour un homosexuel pour débusquer un tueur en série, il est peu à peu séduit par ce mode de vie qui lui était étranger.

PORTRAIT FOR 'CRUISING' (1980)
At the time, homosexuality was a risky topic for any movie star to take on, but Pacino embraced the challenge. / Damals war Homosexualität für einen Filmstar noch ein riskantes Thema, doch Pacino stellte sich der Herausforderung. / Bien que l'homosexualité constitue à l'époque un sujet à risque pour une star de cinéma, Al Pacino relève bravement le défi.

STILL FROM 'CRUISING' (1980)
A watchful man, suffering in isolation—these qualities
would seem to sum up the art of Al Pacino at his most
memorable. / Ein wachsamer Mensch, der an seiner
Isolation leidet - so könnte man Al Pacinos Kunst in
seinen denkwürdigsten Momenten zusammenfassend
beschreiben. / Un homme aux aguets, souffrant en
silence : des caractéristiques qui résument bien le
personnage d'Al Pacino au sommet de son art.

ON THE SET OF 'CRUISING' (1980)
Pacino with director William Friedkin (*The French
Connection, The Exorcist*), who conjures a terrifying
psychological atmosphere. / Pacino mit Regisseur
William Friedkin (*Brennpunkt Brooklyn, Der Exorzist*),
der eine Furcht einflößende psychologische
Atmosphäre heraufbeschwört. / Pacino et le réalisateur
William Friedkin (*French Connection, L'Exorciste*), qui
instaure une atmosphère psychologique terrifiante.

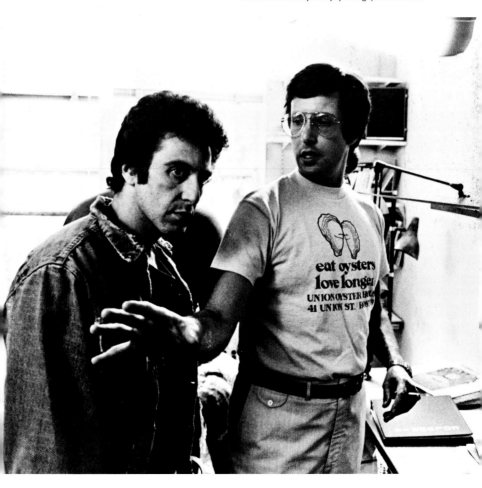

STILL FROM 'AUTHOR! AUTHOR!' (1982)
The playwright makes love to the leading lady (Dyan
Cannon). Pacino lightly navigates many moods in this
funny, intelligent film. / Der Dramaturg wird mit der
Hauptdarstellerin seines Stücks (Dyan Cannon) intim.
Pacino bahnt sich in diesem witzigen und intelligenten
Film seinen Weg durch eine Vielzahl von Stimmungen. /
Dans ce film drôle et intelligent où il incarne un
dramaturge épris de son actrice principale (Dyan
Cannon), Pacino décline avec finesse toute une
palette d'émotions.

Lawrence Grobel: *"If you could have selected
your biographer, what writer would do you
justice?"*
Al Pacino: *"Dostoyevsky. Though he's not
a lot of laughs."*

Lawrence Grobel: „Wenn Sie sich Ihren Biografen
hätten aussuchen können, welcher Schriftsteller
würde Ihnen gerecht?"
Al Pacino: „Dostojewski. Obwohl es dann nicht viel
zu lachen gäbe."

STILL FROM 'AUTHOR! AUTHOR!' (1982)
This family comedy stars Pacino as renowned
playwright Ivan Travalian, from a screenplay by
renowned playwright Israel Horovitz. / In dieser
Familienkomödie nach dem Drehbuch des berühmten
Dramaturgen Israel Horovitz spielt Pacino einen
berühmten Dramaturgen namens Ivan Travalian. / Écrit
par le célèbre dramaturge Israel Horovitz, le scénario de
cette comédie familiale raconte l'histoire... d'un célèbre
dramaturge, Ivan Travalian (Pacino).

Lawrence Grobel : « *Si vous pouviez choisir votre
biographe, quel écrivain vous conviendrait ?* »
Al Pacino : « *Dostoïevski. Même s'il n'est pas très
marrant.* »

STILL FROM 'AUTHOR! AUTHOR!' (1982)
At a pause during rehearsals, Ivan confers with his ever-nervous producers (Bob Dishy, left, and Alan King, right). / Während einer Pause bei den Proben bespricht sich Ivan mit seinen stets nervösen Produzenten (Bob Dishy, links, und Alan King, rechts). / Lors d'une pause durant les répétitions, Ivan discute avec son metteur en scène (Bob Dishy, à gauche) et son producteur hyperanxieux (Alan King, à droite).

STILL FROM 'AUTHOR! AUTHOR!' (1982)
Tuesday Weld (a love of Pacino's in real life) as Ivan's reckless first wife, who leaves the children on his doorstep long after their divorce. / Tuesday Weld (eine von Pacinos Lebensabschnittsgefährtinnen) spielt Ivans skrupellose erste Ehefrau, die lange nach der Scheidung die gemeinsamen Kinder vor seiner Haustür ablädt. / Tuesday Weld (l'une des conquêtes d'Al Pacino dans la vraie vie) incarne l'épouse d'Ivan, une femme irresponsable qui part en abandonnant ses enfants sur le pas de la porte.

STILL FROM 'SCARFACE' (1983)
Yet another iconic role—Tony Montana, Cuban refugee, bare-knuckled climber, American dreamer, nobody to mess with. / Eine weitere Kultrolle: Tony Montana, ein Kubaflüchtling, der den amerikanischen Traum träumt, der sich rücksichtslos seinen Weg nach oben bahnt und mit dem nicht zu scherzen ist. / Al Pacino dans un autre rôle mythique : celui de Tony Montana, réfugié cubain à la poursuite du rêve américain, qui gravit l'échelle sociale à la force du poignet et au prix d'une impitoyable intransigeance.

STILL FROM 'SCARFACE' (1983)
Tony is nearly killed on his first assignment. Brian De
Palma directs this particular sequence with a nerve-
torturing gusto. / Sein erster Auftrag kostet Tony
beinahe das Leben. Brian De Palma inszenierte diese
spezielle Szene mit nervenzerreißendem Gusto. /
Lorsque Tony frôle la mort durant sa première mission,
le réalisateur Brian De Palma se complaît à jouer avec
les nerfs du spectateur.

STILL FROM 'SCARFACE' (1983)
Although simple and self-educated—"I grew up watching movies"—Tony is uncannily smart about power, and how to attain it. / Wenngleich er ein Autodidakt – „Ich wuchs mit dem Kino auf" – von schlichtem Gemüt ist, weiß Tony, wie man Macht erlangt und damit umgeht. / Autodidacte issu d'un milieu simple (« J'ai grandi en regardant des films »), Tony possède une extraordinaire intelligence du pouvoir et des moyens d'y parvenir.

STILL FROM 'SCARFACE' (1983)
Tony taunts his enemies by introducing them to his rifle:
"Say hello to my little friend." / Tony verspottet seine
Feinde, indem er ihnen seine Knarre vorstellt: „Sag
meinem kleinen Freund hier Guten Tag!" / Tony nargue
ses ennemis en leur présentant son fusil : « Dis bonjour
à mon pote. »

STILL FROM 'SCARFACE' (1983)
"Top of the World," as his closest friend and fellow climber (Steven Bauer, left) looks on. / Auf dem „Gipfel der Welt", während sein engster Freund (Steven Bauer, links), der den Aufstieg mit ihm teilte, zuschaut. / Tony au «sommet du monde» sous le regard de son meilleur ami (Steven Bauer, à gauche), complice de son ascension.

PORTRAIT FOR 'SCARFACE' (1983)
The smoldering intensity is familiar, as is that all-seeing gaze, but Pacino takes care never to repeat himself. Tony is uniquely Tony. / Die schwelende Intensität des Films ist ebenso vertraut wie dieser Blick, der alles sieht, doch Pacino achtet darauf, sich nicht zu wiederholen. Tony ist einzig und allein Tony. / Si l'on reconnaît son intensité brûlante et son regard vigilant, Pacino prend soin de ne jamais se répéter. Tony ne ressemble à personne.

STILL FROM 'SCARFACE' (1983)
"Mr. Big Shot" on his throne in a moment of reflection—
the only way out is down. / "Mr. Big Shot" in einem
nachdenklichen Augenblick auf seinem Thron - von hier
aus kann es nur abwärts gehen. / Le « grand manitou »
sur son trône, perdu dans ses pensées : on ne sort d'ici
que par le bas.

STILL FROM 'SCARFACE' (1983)

As his trophy wife, Elvira—the first major role of her career—Michelle Pfeiffer (left) favors Tony with her honest opinion of him. / Elvira, die Ehefrau, die Tony wie eine Trophäe behandelt – Michelle Pfeiffer in ihrer ersten großen Filmrolle –, sagt Tony in dieser Szene ganz ehrlich, was sie von ihm hält. / Dans le rôle d'Elvira, sa « femme trophée » (le premier grand rôle de sa carrière), Michelle Pfeiffer (à gauche) ne cache pas à Tony ce qu'elle pense de lui.

PAGES 88/89
STILL FROM 'SCARFACE' (1983)

Oliver Stone's screenplay, derived from the 1930s classic written by Ben Hecht, very much goes its own way, as does its protagonist. / Oliver Stones Drehbuch nach dem Klassiker von Ben Hecht aus den 1930er-Jahren geht größtenteils eigene Wege – genau wie der Protagonist. / Tiré d'un roman des années 1930 écrit par Ben Hecht, le scénario d'Oliver Stone suit sa propre voie, tout comme son personnage principal.

STILL FROM 'REVOLUTION' (1985)
A fine performance, in an underrated film: Tom Dobb
(Pacino) fights to protect his son's life in the America of
the 1770s. / Eine gute Leistung in einem
unterbewerteten Film: Tom Dobb (Pacino) kämpft im
Amerika der 1770er-Jahre, um das Leben seines Sohnes
zu schützen. / Une remarquable interprétation dans un
film sous-évalué : Tom Dobb (Pacino) se bat pour
protéger son fils dans l'Amérique des années 1770.

*"I hate to be married to one idea.
I'm a philosophical anarchist."*
Al Pacino

*„Ich hasse es, mit einer Idee verheiratet zu sein.
Ich bin ein philosophischer Anarchist."*
Al Pacino

*« Je déteste épouser une idée. Sur le plan
philosophique, je suis un anarchiste. »*
Al Pacino

STILL FROM 'REVOLUTION' (1985)
Robert Dillon wrote, and Hugh Hudson directed, this
visually handsome epic tapestry. There are few close-
ups—a deliberate choice. / Robert Dillon schrieb das
Buch, und Hugh Hudson führte Regie bei diesem visuell
bestechenden epischen Gemälde. Dass es nur wenige
Nahaufnahmen gab, war eine bewusste Entscheidung. /
Écrite par Robert Dillon et mise en scène par Hugh
Hudson, cette splendide épopée évite délibérément
les gros plans.

STILL FROM 'REVOLUTION' (1985)
Tenderness with a partisan in the American cause, Nastassja Kinski. Pacino felt strongly that the film was rushed, unfinished, into release. / Hier tauscht er Zärtlichkeiten mit Daisy (Nastassja Kinski) aus, die für die aufständischen Kolonisten Partei ergriffen hat. Pacino hatte das Gefühl, der Film sei unfertig und übereilt in die Kinos gebracht worden. / Scène de tendresse avec une partisane de la cause américaine (Nastassja Kinski) dans un film qu'Al Pacino estime avoir été bâclé pour hâter sa sortie.

PORTRAIT FOR 'REVOLUTION' (1985)
The original goal had been to make a film almost entirely without words. Certainly Pacino's eyes speak volumes. / Ursprünglich sollte der Film fast gänzlich ohne Worte auskommen. Pacinos Augen sprachen gewiss Bände. / Dans ce film, qui devait à l'origine être presque entièrement dénué de dialogues, le regard d'Al Pacino en dit plus qu'un long discours.

STILL FROM 'SEA OF LOVE' (1989)
After a four-year absence from the screen, which he
devoted to stage work, Pacino returned in strength
with this unexpected hit. / Nach einer vierjährigen
Kinopause, in der er nur auf der Bühne gestanden hatte,
kehrte Pacino mit einer starken Leistung in diesem
Überraschungshit auf die Leinwand zurück. / Après
quatre ans d'absence consacrés au théâtre, Al Pacino
revient en force avec ce succès inattendu.

PORTRAIT FOR 'SEA OF LOVE' (1989)
The lonely vigilance of this police detective attracts this
exceptional woman (Ellen Barkin), but is she or is she
not a murderer? / Die Wachsamkeit des einsamen
Kripobeamten wirkt auf diese außergewöhnliche Frau
(Ellen Barkin) anziehend – doch ist sie eine Mörderin
oder nicht? / Attirée par la vigilance solitaire de
l'inspecteur Keller, cette femme exceptionnelle
(Ellen Barkin) est-elle ou non la meurtrière ?

STILL FROM 'SEA OF LOVE' (1989)
With his fellow detective in the search for the killer
(John Goodman, left). A low-key moment of humor
between partners. / Mit seinem Kollegen (John
Goodman, links) auf der Suche nach dem Mörder:
Die Partner genießen einen kurzen Augenblick der
Heiterkeit. / Moment de détente en compagnie de son
collègue (John Goodman, à gauche), avec lequel il tente
de retrouver la trace du tueur.

STILL FROM 'SEA OF LOVE' (1989)
Richard Price's intricate, psychologically subtle
screenplay and Harold Becker's solid direction brought
out Pacino at his best. / Das verzwickte und psycholo-
gisch subtile Drehbuch von Richard Price sowie Harold
Beckers solide Regie brachten Pacinos stärkste Seiten
zum Vorschein. / Alliée à la subtilité psychologique du
scénario de Richard Price, la solide direction d'acteur
de Harold Becker donne le meilleur d'Al Pacino.

PORTRAIT FOR 'DICK TRACY' (1990)
This gallery of rubber-faced crooks derives from the
imagination of cartoonist Chester Gould—but sends up
The Godfather, too. / Diese Galerie gummigesichtiger
Schurken entstammte der Phantasie des
Comiczeichners Chester Gould – und parodierte
nebenher den *Paten*. / Avec leurs mines improbables
tout droit sorties de l'imagination de l'auteur de BD
Chester Gould, ces bandits en smoking ne sont pas
sans rappeler *Le Parrain*.

STILL FROM 'DICK TRACY' (1990)
Big Boy Caprice—an opportunity handed down from
movie heaven for Pacino to spoof himself. Madonna
(right) is his girlfriend. / Die Rolle des Big Boy Caprice
war ein Geschenk des Himmels für Pacino, das ihm die
Gelegenheit gab, sich selbst durch den Kakao zu ziehen.
Madonna (rechts) spielt hier die Gangsterbraut. /
Le personnage de Big Boy Caprice, ici aux côtés de sa
petite amie (Madonna), offre à Al Pacino une occasion
inespérée de s'auto-parodier.

**STILL FROM
'THE GODFATHER: PART III' (1990)**
The third godfather in the trinity, Andy Garcia (left),
poised to assume the power about to be bequeathed
by Michael (center). / Der dritte Pate des Dreigestirns,
Andy Garcia (links), nimmt die Macht an, die ihm
Michael (Mitte) verleiht. / Le troisième parrain de la
trinité, incarné par Andy Garcia (à gauche), s'apprête à
hériter du pouvoir légué par Michael (au centre).

**PORTRAIT FOR
'THE GODFATHER: PART III' (1990)**
"When I first read Puzo's novel *The Godfather*," Francis
Ford Coppola recalled later, "I saw Al as Michael." This
is how icons are born. / „Als ich Puzos Roman *Der Pate*
zum ersten Mal las", erinnerte sich Francis Ford
Coppola später, „sah ich Al als Michael." So entstehen
Kultfiguren. / La naissance d'un mythe : « Quand j'ai lu le
roman de Puzo intitulé *Le Parrain* », racontera plus tard
Francis Ford Coppola, « j'ai tout de suite vu Al dans le
rôle de Michael. »

**STILL FROM
'THE GODFATHER: PART III' (1990)**
"I didn't know if I could be that guy again," Pacino
confessed of this role. What appealed to him was the
"maturity" of this fresh take. / „Ich wusste nicht, ob ich
noch einmal dieser Typ sein konnte", gestand Pacino

bezüglich der Rolle. Was ihn reizte, war die „Reife"
dieser Fortführung. / « Je ne savais pas si je pourrais de
nouveau endosser ce rôle », confesse Al Pacino, séduit
par la « maturité » acquise par son personnage.

ON THE SET OF
'THE GODFATHER: PART III' (1990)
A laugh between takes with Diane Keaton (right). In the span between *The Godfather: Part II* and *Part III*, they had for a time been lovers in real life. / Ein Scherz in der Drehpause mit Diane Keaton (rechts). In der Zeit zwischen dem Dreh des zweiten und dritten Teils der Trilogie waren die beiden im wahren Leben vorübergehend ein Paar gewesen. / Moment de détente entre les prises avec Diane Keaton (à droite). Entre le tournage du deuxième et du troisième volet de la trilogie, les deux acteurs ont été amants dans la vraie vie.

PAGES 104/105
STILL FROM
'THE GODFATHER: PART III' (1990)
The death of Don Vito in *The Godfather* involved the hull of a peeled orange. For Michael, death is the whole fruit. / Beim Tod Don Vitos in *Der Pate* spielte die Schale einer Orange eine Rolle. Für Michael wird die ganze Frucht zum Todessymbol. / Dans le premier volet du *Parrain*, la mort de Don Vito était associée à une écorce d'orange. Pour Michael, c'est le fruit entier qui symbolise la mort.

STILL FROM 'FRANKIE AND JOHNNY' (1991)
Pacino enjoys improvising in rehearsal, when
circumstances and his creative partners permit, but
Pfeiffer preferred not to. / Pacino macht es Spaß, bei
den Proben zu improvisieren, wenn es die Umstände
und seine kreativen Partner zulassen, doch Pfeiffer hielt
sich lieber an ihren Text. / Si Al Pacino aime improviser
pendant les répétitions lorsque les circonstances et ses
partenaires le permettent, ce n'est pas le cas de
Michelle Pfeiffer.

STILL FROM 'FRANKIE AND JOHNNY' (1991)
Bringing Terrence McNally's hit play to the screen
reunited Pacino with Michelle Pfeiffer (left), by now a
big star in her own right. / In der Verfilmung von
Terrence McNallys erfolgreichem Bühnenstück stand
Pacino wieder mit Michelle Pfeiffer (links) gemeinsam
vor der Kamera, die inzwischen selbst ein großer
Star geworden war. / L'adaptation de la pièce à succès
de Terrence McNally réunit à nouveau Al Pacino et
Michelle Pfeiffer (à gauche), devenue elle aussi une star.

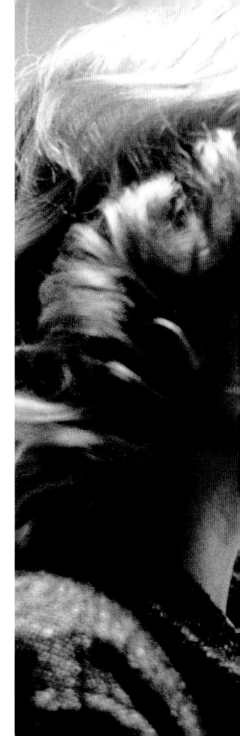

"There's no such thing as happiness, only
concentration. When you're concentrated, you're
happy. Also, when you're not thinking of yourself
a lot, you're happy."
Al Pacino

„So etwas wie Glück gibt es nicht, [es gibt] nur
Konzentration. Wenn man sich konzentriert, ist
man glücklich. Und wenn man nicht viel an sich
selbst denkt, ist man auch glücklich."
Al Pacino

« Je ne crois pas au bonheur, seulement à la
concentration. Quand on est concentré, on est
heureux. Quand on ne pense pas trop à soi,
on est heureux. »
Al Pacino

STILL FROM 'FRANKIE AND JOHNNY' (1991)
The play describes a pair of lonely characters who are
physically plain and beautified by their love—but, hello,
this is Hollywood. / Das Stück beschreibt ein Paar, das
aus zwei einsamen und äußerlich eher unscheinbaren
Menschen besteht, deren Schönheit erst durch ihre
Liebe zueinander aufblüht, aber – schließlich sind wir
ja hier in Hollywood! / La pièce de théâtre met en
scène deux personnages solitaires au physique assez
banal que seul l'amour rend beaux... Chose impensable
à Hollywood!

STILL FROM 'GLENGARRY GLEN ROSS' (1992)
In the circle of hell described by David Mamet's Pulitzer Prize–winning play, Ricky Roma (Pacino) is the only successful salesman. / In dem Höllenkreis, den David Mamet in seinem mit dem Pulitzerpreis ausgezeichneten Stück beschreibt, ist Ricky Roma (Pacino) der einzige Handelsvertreter, der Erfolg hat. / Dans le cercle infernal décrit par la pièce de David Mamet (récompensée par le prix Pulitzer), Ricky Roma (Pacino) est le seul vendeur à réussir au sein de l'entreprise.

"The less you want things, the more they come to you. If it's meant to be, it will be."
Al Pacino

„Je weniger du dir Dinge wünschst, desto eher kommen sie zu dir. Wenn es sein soll, dann wird es sein."
Al Pacino

« Moins vous désirez les choses, plus elles viennent à vous. Si ça doit se faire, ça se fera. »
Al Pacino

STILL FROM 'GLENGARRY GLEN ROSS' (1992)
Ricky spends the better part of a night wooing a "yes"
out of Jonathan Pryce (right), and appears to have no
other private life. / Ricky verbringt den größten Teil
einer Nacht damit, James (Jonathan Pryce, rechts) ein
„Ja" zu entlocken, und scheint ansonsten kein
Privatleben zu besitzen. / Apparemment dénué de vie
privée, Ricky passe une bonne partie de la nuit à
extorquer un « oui » à Jonathan Pryce (à droite).

STILL FROM 'SCENT OF A WOMAN' (1992)
Chris O'Donnell (left) is the university student obliged to "babysit" the blind Frank—only to have his own eyes opened, to life. / Chris O'Donnell (links) spielt den Studenten, der den blinden Frank „babysitten" muss – und dem dabei selbst die Augen geöffnet werden, und zwar für das Leben. / Chris O'Donnell (à gauche) est un étudiant chargé de « garder » le temps d'un week-end un officier aveugle qui finira par lui ouvrir les yeux sur la vie.

STILL FROM 'SCENT OF A WOMAN' (1992)
As retired Lieutenant Colonel Frank Slade, blinded during his tour of Vietnam, dancing a grand tango with a young beauty (Gabrielle Anwar). / Als Frank Slade, ein Oberstleutnant im Ruhestand, der bei seinem Einsatz in Vietnam sein Augenlicht verlor, tanzt Pacino mit einer jungen Schönheit (Gabrielle Anwar) Tango. / Dans le rôle de Frank Slade, lieutenant-colonel à la retraite devenu aveugle au Viêtnam, Al Pacino danse un tango endiablé avec une jeune beauté (Gabrielle Anwar).

STILL FROM 'CARLITO'S WAY' (1993)
Lawyer David Kleinfeld (Sean Penn, left) sprang Carlito
(Pacino) from prison, but he has an agenda of his own
and won't let Carlito go straight. / Rechtsanwalt David
Kleinfeld (Sean Penn, links) holte Carlito (Pacino) aus
dem Gefängnis, doch er verfolgt seine eigenen Pläne
und gibt Carlito keine Chance, auf den rechten Weg
zurückzufinden. / Bien qu'il l'ait fait sortir de prison,
l'avocat David Kleinfeld (Sean Penn, à gauche) ne laisse
pas Carlito (Al Pacino) rentrer dans le droit chemin,
car il a d'autres projets.

PORTRAIT FOR 'CARLITO'S WAY' (1993)
Despite sharing a profession with Michael Corleone
and Tony Montana, Carlito is by contrast a man of
honor. / Obwohl er den gleichen „Beruf" ausübt wie
Michael Corleone und Tony Montana, ist Carlito im
Vergleich zu diesen Figuren ein Ehrenmann. / Bien qu'il
exerce le même «métier» que Michael Corleone et
Tony Montana, Carlito est un homme d'honneur en
comparaison.

STILL FROM 'CARLITO'S WAY' (1993)
Carlito makes one final, desperate attempt to leave
his old criminal life behind, but he cannot escape his
past. / Carlito unternimmt einen letzten verzweifelten
Versuch, sein altes Verbrecherleben hinter sich zu
lassen, doch er kann seiner Vergangenheit nicht
entkommen. / Malgré une dernière tentative
désespérée pour fuir son existence criminelle,
Carlito ne parvient pas à échapper à son passé.

STILL FROM 'CARLITO'S WAY' (1993)
Carlito's dreams of a new life after leaving prison
include reuniting with Gail (Penelope Ann Miller), the
dancer he loved before. / In Carlitos Träumen von
einem neuen Leben nach der Gefängnisstrafe möchte
er auch die Tänzerin Gail (Penelope Ann Miller)
zurückgewinnen, die er zuvor geliebt hatte. / À sa
sortie de prison, Carlito rêve de refaire sa vie avec
son ancienne compagne, la danseuse Gail (Penelope
Ann Miller).

STILL FROM 'TWO BITS' (1995)
"The image of my grandfather," Pacino said of this role.
"This isn't who he was, but if I could paint, this is how I
would paint him." / „Das Abbild meines Großvaters",
meinte Pacino zu dieser Rolle. „So ist er nicht gewesen,
aber wenn ich malen könnte, dann würde ich ihn so
malen." / « L'image de mon grand-père », confie Al
Pacino au sujet de ce rôle. « Ce n'est pas ainsi qu'il était,
mais si je savais peindre, c'est ainsi que je le peindrais. »

ON THE SET OF 'TWO BITS' (1995)
James Foley (left), who directed *Glengarry Glen Ross*,
invited Pacino to play a much older man here, and
Pacino relished the challenge. / James Foley (links), der
Regisseur von *Glengarry Glen Ross*, lud Pacino ein, hier
einen wesentlich älteren Mann zu spielen, und Pacino
genoss die Herausforderung. / James Foley (à gauche),
le réalisateur de *Glengarry*, lui propose le rôle d'un
homme beaucoup plus âgé ; Pacino relève le défi.

STILL FROM 'HEAT' (1995)
With Robert De Niro (right). "We weren't dueling banjos," says Pacino. "We were in it together, trying to bring off the moment." / Mit Robert De Niro (rechts).

„Wir wollten uns nicht gegenseitig überbieten", sagte Pacino. „Wir steckten zusammen drin und versuchten, den Augenblick zur Geltung zu bringen." / Avec Robert

De Niro (à droite). « Ce n'était pas un duel », déclare
Al Pacino. « Nous avons uni nos forces pour tenter de
mettre cet instant en valeur. »

PORTRAIT FOR 'HEAT' (1995)
Diane Venora plays Hanna's long-suffering third wife; she later played a similar role opposite Russell Crowe in *The Insider*. / Diane Venora spielt Hannas langmütige dritte Ehefrau. Später spielte sie eine ähnliche Rolle an der Seite von Russell Crowe in *Insider*. / Diane Venora incarne la troisième femme de Hanna, un rôle d'épouse délaissée qu'elle retrouvera aux côtés de Russell Crowe dans *Révélations*.

STILL FROM 'HEAT' (1995)
"You are what you hunt," it is said of Vincent Hanna (Pacino), this ultra-dedicated detective. Pacino is ideally suited to project this man's deliberate solitude. / „Du bist, was du jagst", heißt es von Vincent Hanna (Pacino), diesem extrem pflichtbewussten Kripobeamten. Pacino ist die Idealbesetzung, um die selbst auferlegte Einsamkeit dieses Menschen zu vermitteln. / «Je suis ce que je poursuis», déclare Vincent Hanna, policier entièrement dévoué à son métier dont Al Pacino reflète parfaitement la solitude assumée.

"It's like you said. All I am is what I'm going after."
Lieutenant Vincent Hanna, *Heat* (1995)

„Es ist so, wie Sie gesagt haben: Alles, was ich bin,
ist das, hinter dem ich her bin."
Lieutenant Vincent Hanna, *Heat* (1995)

« Tu as raison. Je suis ce que je poursuis. »
Lieutenant Vincent Hanna, *Heat* (1995)

STILL FROM 'HEAT' (1995)
An extraordinary sequence, in which a quiet city
street erupts into literal warfare against crime. /
Eine außergewöhnliche Sequenz, in der in einer ruhigen
Stadtstraße der Krieg gegen das Verbrechen in seiner
vollen Härte ausbricht. / Séquence extraordinaire
durant laquelle une rue paisible se transforme en
véritable champ de bataille.

STILL FROM 'CITY HALL' (1995)
A big-city mayor (Pacino) enjoys renown as an idealist,
until he is investigated by a more genuine idealist (John
Cusack, right). / Der Bürgermeister einer Großstadt
(Pacino) genießt seinen Ruf als Idealist, bis er von einem
ernsthafteren Idealisten (John Cusack, rechts) unter die
Lupe genommen wird. / Maire d'une grande ville, John
Pappas (Pacino) est réputé pour son idéalisme jusqu'à
ce qu'un collègue (John Cusack, à droite), plus idéaliste
encore, se mette à enquêter sur lui.

STILL FROM 'CITY HALL' (1995)
Mayor Pappas turns a funeral to his advantage: "The first and perhaps only great mayor was Greek. He was Pericles of Athens ... " / Bürgermeister Pappas nutzt eine Beerdigung zum eigenen Vorteil: „Der erste und vielleicht einzige große Bürgermeister war ein Grieche. Es war Perikles von Athen ... " / John Pappas profite d'un enterrement pour se mettre en valeur : « Le premier et peut-être le seul grand maire de l'histoire était grec. C'était Périclès à Athènes... »

STILL FROM 'LOOKING FOR RICHARD' (1996)
Directed by Pacino himself, who also stars, this merry mix of documentary and Shakespeare adaptation was many years in the making. / Es dauerte viele Jahre, bis diese fröhliche Mischung aus Dokumentarfilm und Shakespeare-Verfilmung, bei der Pacino selbst Regie führte, endlich „im Kasten" war. / Réalisé et interprété par Al Pacino en personne, ce joyeux mélange de séquences documentaires et d'une adaptation de Shakespeare a demandé plusieurs années de préparation.

**ON THE SET OF
'LOOKING FOR RICHARD' (1996)**
Staged largely at The Cloisters—a landmark of Manhattan—the cast includes Kevin Spacey (center), Alec Baldwin, and Winona Ryder. / Der Film wurde hauptsächlich in "The Cloisters" gedreht, einem mittelalterlichen Museum im Norden Manhattans. Zur Besetzung zählten Kevin Spacey (Mitte), Alec Baldwin und Winona Ryder. / Principalement tourné aux Cloisters, l'une des curiosités de Manhattan, ce film met notamment en scène Kevin Spacey (au centre), Alec Baldwin et Winona Ryder.

STILL FROM 'DONNIE BRASCO' (1997)
Johnny Depp (left), in one of his best performances, is FBI man Donnie Brasco pretending to befriend aging, low-level mobster Benjamin "Lefty" Ruggiero (Pacino). / Johnny Depp (links) gibt eine seiner besten schauspielerischen Leistungen in der Rolle des FBI-Agenten Donnie Brasco, der vorgibt, sich mit dem alternden Kleinmafioso Benjamin "Lefty" Ruggiero (Pacino) anzufreunden. / Johnny Depp (à gauche), remarquable dans le rôle de Donnie Brasco, un agent du FBI chargé d'infiltrer la mafia en se liant avec Benjamin Ruggiero alias « Lefty » (Pacino), un second couteau vieillissant et aigri.

PAGES 130/131
**ON THE SET OF
'LOOKING FOR RICHARD' (1996)**
"My kingdom for a horse!" ... At momentary ease while filming the tumultuous downfall of Richard III. / „Mein Königreich für ein Pferd!" ... Eine Drehpause bringt vorübergehende Entspannung in die Verfilmung des turbulenten Untergangs König Richards III. / « Mon royaume pour un cheval ! » Moment de détente pendant le tournage de la chute tumultueuse de Richard III.

STILL FROM 'DONNIE BRASCO' (1997)
At a certain level of intimacy, their friendship becomes real, even for the cop. Pacino's thug is too authentically kind to despise. / Auf einer bestimmten Ebene wird die Freundschaft der beiden Wirklichkeit – sogar für den Polizisten. So freundlich, wie Pacino den Gangster spielt, kann man ihn nicht wirklich verabscheuen. / Trop sincère et dévoué pour inspirer le mépris, Lefty atteint un tel degré d'intimité avec Donnie que le flic et le truand se lient réellement d'amitié.

"Thirty years I'm busting my hump.
What have I got? ... Who the fuck am I? Who am I?
I'm a spoke on a wheel."
Benjamin "Lefty" Ruggiero, *Donnie Brasco* (1997)

„Dreißig Jahre lang reiß' ich mir den Arsch auf. Und
was hab ich davon? ... Wer zum Teufel bin ich? Wer
bin ich? Ich bin eine Speiche im Rad."
Benjamin "Lefty" Ruggiero, *Donnie Brasco* (1997)

« Trente ans que je me casse le cul. Et qu'est-ce que
j'ai ? [...] Qui je suis ? Qui je suis, bon sang ? Je suis
un maillon dans la chaîne. »
Benjamin Ruggiero alias « Lefty », *Donnie Brasco* (1997)

STILL FROM 'DONNIE BRASCO' (1997)
Donnie never loses sight of his lawful duties, and he may
even have to destroy Lefty—but he doesn't want to. /
Donnie verliert nie seine Dienstpflicht aus dem Blick,
auch wenn er dafür Leftys Leben zerstören müsste –
was er aber nicht möchte. / Ne perdant jamais de
vue son devoir, Donnie sait qu'il devra peut-être
– à contrecœur – se débarrasser de Lefty.

PORTRAIT FOR 'DONNIE BRASCO' (1997)
The role of Lefty Ruggiero is poignant by definition—
trusting, loyal—but Pacino lights deep layers of insight as
few actors could. / Schon von ihrer Anlage her ist die
Rolle des Lefty Ruggiero – zutraulich und loyal –
ergreifend, doch Pacino eröffnet weitere tiefe Einblicke
in die Figur, wie es nur wenige Schauspieler fertig-
gebracht hätten. / Si le personnage naïf et loyal de Lefty
Ruggiero est poignant par essence, Al Pacino lui
apporte une richesse et une profondeur dont peu
d'acteurs seraient capables.

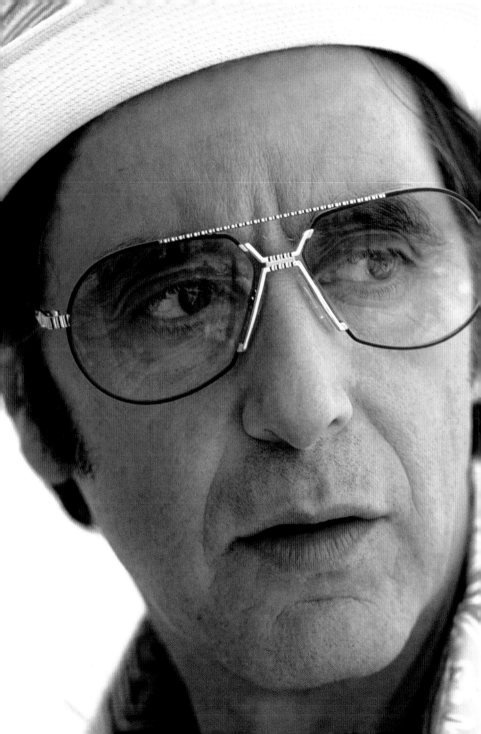

STILL FROM 'THE DEVIL'S ADVOCATE' (1997)
Pacino is a funny, charismatic Satan—should we be
surprised? / Pacino ist ein witziger, charismatischer
Satan - sollte uns das überraschen? / Sous les traits
d'Al Pacino, Satan devient drôle et charismatique... qui
s'en étonnerait ?

POSTER FOR 'THE DEVIL'S ADVOCATE' (1997)
Incarnating the Devil himself for director Taylor
Hackford, in a film cowritten by Tony Gilroy (*Michael
Clayton, The Bourne Identity*). / Für Regisseur Taylor
Hackford spielt er den Teufel höchstpersönlich in
einem Film, dessen Drehbuch unter anderem von
Tony Gilroy (*Michael Clayton, Die Bourne Identität*)
verfasst wurde. / Al Pacino incarne le diable en
personne sous la direction de Taylor Hackford, dans
un film co-écrit par Tony Gilroy (*Michael Clayton,
La Mémoire dans la peau*).

PAGES 138/139
STILL FROM 'THE DEVIL'S ADVOCATE' (1997)
Keanu Reeves (left) is the lawyer of great promise who
slowly realizes just who his boss is. Here, he is being
offered the world. / Keanu Reeves (links) spielt den
vielversprechenden Rechtsanwalt, der allmählich
begreift, wer sein Chef ist. Hier legt dieser ihm die Welt
zu Füßen. / Jeune avocat prometteur, Kevin Lomax
(Keanu Reeves, à gauche) découvre peu à peu la
véritable identité de son employeur, qui lui propose
ici d'avoir le monde à ses pieds.

*"Underestimated from day one. You'd never think
I was a master of the universe, now would ya?"*
John Milton (Satan), *The Devil's Advocate* (1997)

*„Vom ersten Tag an unterschätzt. Sie hätten nicht
gedacht, dass ich ein Meister des Universums bin,
oder?"*
John Milton (Satan), *Im Auftrag des Teufels* (1997)

*« Sous-estimé dès le départ. Sans blague, qui se
douterait que je suis un des maîtres de l'univers ? »*
John Milton (Satan), *L'Associé du diable* (1997)

STILL FROM 'THE DEVIL'S ADVOCATE' (1997)
Few actors can explode louder, or with greater
conviction, than this man. Few directors can resist
asking him to do exactly that. / Es gibt nur wenige
Schauspieler, die lauter oder überzeugender
explodieren können als dieser Mensch. Und nur wenige
Regisseure können es sich verkneifen, ihn genau das
tun zu lassen. / Rares sont les acteurs capables
d'exploser avec autant de violence et de conviction.
Rares sont les réalisateurs capables de se priver d'un
tel bonheur.

STILL FROM 'THE INSIDER' (1999)
Opposite Russell Crowe (right), once again under the
direction of Michael Mann—a masterly, subtle,
nonexplosive performance. / Neben Russell Crowe
(rechts) und erneut unter der Regie von Michael Mann
- eine meisterhaft subtile und gar nicht explosive
Schauspielleistung. / Aux côtés de Russell Crowe
(à droite), Al Pacino se retrouve sous la direction de
Michael Mann pour une interprétation magistrale,
tout en subtilité et en retenue.

STILL FROM 'THE INSIDER' (1999)
The story is true. Pacino plays journalist Lowell
Bergman, fighting corporate corruption in the tobacco
and news industries. / Die Geschichte ist wahr. Pacino
spielt den Journalisten Lowell Bergman, der gegen
Korruption in der Wirtschaft ankämpft – sowohl in der
Tabakindustrie als auch in den Nachrichtenmedien. /
L'histoire vraie du journaliste Lowell Bergman (Pacino),
parti en croisade contre la corruption de l'industrie du
tabac et des médias.

AL PACINO   RUSSELL CROWE

A Michael Mann Film

THE INSIDER

ON THE SET OF 'THE INSIDER' (1999)
The two actors pose here with the actual men they
represent on film: Jeffrey Wigand (left) and Lowell
Bergman (right). / Die beiden Schauspieler posieren
hier mit den Männern, die sie im Film darstellen: Jeffrey
Wigand (links) und Lowell Bergman (rechts). / Les deux
acteurs posant aux côtés des deux hommes qu'ils
incarnent à l'écran : Jeffrey Wigand (à gauche) et
Lowell Bergman (à droite).

POSTER FOR 'THE INSIDER' (1999)
Pacino (above) and Crowe (below) are talents as
well matched as two prizefighters, as are the men they
play. / Pacino (oben) und Crowe (unten) sind zwei
Talente, die so gut zueinander passen wie zwei
Preisboxer – und das trifft auch auf die Männer zu, die
sie spielen. / Pacino (en haut) et Crowe (en bas), deux
talents aussi bien assortis que les personnages qu'ils
interprètent.

"On any given Sunday you're gonna win or you're gonna lose. The point is—can you win or lose like a man?"
Coach Tony D'Amato, *Any Given Sunday* (1999)

„An jedem verdammten Sonntag gewinnt man oder verliert man. Wichtig ist nur: Kannst du wie ein Mann gewinnen oder verlieren?"
Coach Tony D'Amato, *An jedem verdammten Sonntag* (1999)

« Tous les dimanches, tu vas gagner ou tu vas perdre. La question, c'est de savoir si tu es capable de gagner ou de perdre comme un homme. »
Coach Tony D'Amato, *L'Enfer du dimanche* (1999)

STILL FROM 'ANY GIVEN SUNDAY' (1999)
As a professional football coach, for director Oliver Stone. His energy makes Pacino tower over men a head taller than him. / Als Coach einer Profi-Football-Mannschaft unter der Regie von Oliver Stone. Durch seine Energie hat Pacino auch Männer im Griff, die einen Kopf größer sind als er selbst. / Dans ce film d'Oliver Stone où il joue un entraîneur de football américain, Al Pacino déploie assez d'énergie pour intimider des hommes d'une tête de plus que lui.

STILL FROM 'ANY GIVEN SUNDAY' (1999)
Consoling a fallen player but never taking his eye off the ball. Pacino is the definition of relentless focus. / Auch als er einem Spieler Trost spendet, verliert der Coach den Ball nicht aus den Augen. Pacino ist der Inbegriff unerschütterlicher Konzentration. / Prenant le temps de consoler un joueur blessé sans jamais perdre de vue le ballon, Al Pacino est l'incarnation absolue d'une concentration sans faille.

STILL FROM 'ANY GIVEN SUNDAY' (1999)
As frivolous as sports may appear to be, Pacino brings to life the dramas of power and leadership that are Stone's perennial themes. / So banal der Sport auch sein mag, Pacino erweckt die Dramen von Macht und Führung zum Leben, die Stones ständige Themen sind. / Malgré l'apparente frivolité du sujet, Al Pacino fait ressortir les enjeux de pouvoir et de domination qui constituent les thèmes de prédilection d'Oliver Stone.

"I can't explain [the parts I choose] in terms of character. There are certain roles that instinctively you connect to, like a note of music or a painting that you see. You have a sort of symbiosis with it."
Al Pacino

„Ich kann [die Rollen, die ich wähle] hinsichtlich der Charaktere nicht erklären. Es gibt bestimmte Rollen, zu denen man instinktiv einen Draht hat, wie zu einer Musiknote oder zu einem Gemälde, das man sieht. Man geht eine Art Symbiose damit ein."
Al Pacino

« Je ne peux pas expliquer [les rôles que je choisis] en termes de personnages. Il y a des rôles avec lesquels on se sent une affinité instinctive, comme avec un tableau ou une note de musique. C'est une sorte de symbiose. »
Al Pacino

ON THE SET OF 'CHINESE COFFEE' (2000)
Pacino at the helm, lining up a shot. The two-character script by Ira Lewis is about the treacheries built into a longtime friendship. / Pacino sucht als Regisseur nach der richtigen Einstellung. Das Drehbuch des Zweipersonenstücks von Ira Lewis handelt von den Tücken einer langjährigen Freundschaft. / Pacino aux commandes, en train de cadrer une prise de vue. Construit autour de deux personnages, le scénario d'Ira Lewis sonde les petits mensonges entre amis.

STILL FROM 'CHINESE COFFEE' (2000)
He has directed several small films, but only released
them on DVD: "They're plays, shot in a movie style." / Er
hat mehrere kleine Filme inszeniert, die jedoch nur auf
DVD veröffentlicht wurden: „Es sind Theaterstücke, die
im Stil eines Films gedreht wurden." / Al Pacino a réalisé
plusieurs petits films qui ne sont sortis qu'en DVD : « Ce
sont des pièces de théâtre filmées comme du cinéma.»

PAGES 154/155
STILL FROM 'INSOMNIA' (2002)
Detective Will Dormer (Pacino) confronts the clever,
wretched, elusive killer Walter Finch (Robin Williams). /
Der Kripobeamte Will Dormer (Pacino) stellt den
schwer fassbaren, cleveren, miesen Mörder Walter
Finch (Robin Williams) zur Rede. / L'inspecteur Will
Dormer (Pacino) aux prises avec Walter Finch (Robin
Williams), tueur aussi intelligent qu'insaisissable.

STILL FROM 'CHINESE COFFEE' (2000)
"I wouldn't call it poetic dialogue," said Pacino, seen
with Jerry Orbach (left). "I would call it amusing—
thought provoking." / „Ich würde es nicht als poetischen
Dialog bezeichnen", sagt Pacino, hier im Bild mit Jerry
Orbach (links). "Ich würde es als unterhaltsam
bezeichnen – als Denkanstoß." / « Je ne qualifierais pas
ces dialogues de poétiques », déclare Al Pacino, ici aux
côtés de Jerry Orbach (à gauche). « Je dirais qu'ils sont
amusants, qu'ils invitent à la réflexion.»

STILL FROM 'INSOMNIA' (2002)
Being rescued by a fellow detective (Hilary Swank).
Pacino placed director Christopher Nolan "in the
category of Michael Mann." / Hier wird er von seiner
Kollegin (Hilary Swank) gerettet. Pacino sah Regisseur
Christopher Nolan „in der gleichen Kategorie wie
Michael Mann". / Dormer est sauvé par sa collègue
(Hilary Swank). Selon Al Pacino, le réalisateur
Christopher Nolan se situe « dans la catégorie de
Michael Mann ».

STILL FROM 'INSOMNIA' (2002)
A sleepless investigator, in the perpetual summer
daylight north of the Arctic Circle. / Ein schlafloser
Ermittler in der ewigen Sommernacht nördlich des
Polarkreises. / Un enquêteur insomniaque dans le jour
sans fin de l'été arctique.

PAGES 158/159
STILL FROM 'S1M0NE' (2002)
Dwarfed by his own creation—film director Viktor
Taransky (Pacino) uses a computer simulation instead of
an actress, and everybody falls in love with her. / Vom
eigenen Geschöpf in den Schatten gestellt: Regisseur
Viktor Taransky (Pacino) setzt eine Computersimulation
anstelle einer Schauspielerin ein, und jeder verliebt sich
in sie. / Le réalisateur Viktor Taransky (Pacino) est
éclipsé par sa propre création, une irrésistible actrice
virtuelle née d'un logiciel de simulation.

STILL FROM 'PEOPLE I KNOW' (2003)
What attracted Kim Basinger (left) and Pacino was the
excellence of the script by playwright Jon Robin Baitz. /
Sowohl Kim Basinger (links) als auch Pacino überzeugte
das hervorragende Drehbuch aus der Feder des
Dramaturgen Jon Robin Baitz. / Kim Basinger (à gauche)
et Al Pacino ont tous deux été attirés par l'excellence
du scénario rédigé par le dramaturge Jon Robin Baitz.

PAGES 162/163
STILL FROM 'THE RECRUIT' (2003)
Walter Burke (Pacino) mentors new CIA agent James
Clayton (Colin Farrell), but are the games real or fake? /
Walter Burke (Pacino) spielt den Mentor des neuen
CIA-Rekruten James Clayton (Colin Farrell) – doch sind
die Spielchen echt oder vorgetäuscht? / Walter Burke
(Pacino) apprend les règles du métier à James Clayton
(Colin Farrell), nouvelle recrue de la CIA. Mais jouent-ils
franc jeu?

STILL FROM 'PEOPLE I KNOW' (2003)
"I saw a great character there," Pacino has recalled.
"But the movie suffered because of a lack of time to do
it." / „Ich erkannte dort eine großartige Figur", erinnert
sich Pacino, „doch der Film litt unter Zeitmangel bei der
Produktion." / « J'y ai vu un excellent personnage,
raconte Al Pacino, mais le film a souffert d'un manque
de temps. »

STILL FROM 'GIGLI' (2003)
With Jennifer Lopez (center left) and Ben Affleck (center right), whose offscreen romance fatally distracted commentators on the resulting film. / Mit Jennifer Lopez (Mitte links) und Ben Affleck (Mitte rechts), deren Liebesverhältnis hinter den Kulissen für mehr Gesprächsstoff sorgte als der Film selbst. / Avec Jennifer Lopez et Ben Affleck (au centre), dont la liaison éclipsera malheureusement le film dans les commentaires des médias.

STILL FROM 'GIGLI' (2003)
"A crazy, disjointed character" is how Pacino described his one-scene contribution to this film by Martin Brest. / Als „eine verrückte, unzusammenhängende Figur" beschrieb Pacino seinen aus einer Szene bestehenden Beitrag zu diesem Film von Martin Brest. / Dans ce film de Martin Brest où il ne joue qu'une seule scène, Pacino incarne ce qu'il appelle « un personnage déglingué ».

STILL FROM 'ANGELS IN AMERICA' (2003)
As Roy Cohn, the right-wing lawyer who died of AIDS:
"Someone alone and defiant. He took comfort and
refuge in being alone." / Als Roy Cohn, der rechte
Rechtsanwalt, der an Aids starb: „Ein einsamer und
trotziger Mensch. Er fand in seiner Einsamkeit Trost
und Zuflucht." / Dans le rôle de Roy Cohn, avocat
réactionnaire mort du sida : « Un homme seul et rebelle,
qui se réfugie dans sa solitude. »

PAGES 168/169
STILL FROM
'THE MERCHANT OF VENICE' (2004)
"I don't see Shylock as comic, or a villain," Pacino has said of his interpretation. "To me, he's a man against the system." / „Ich sehe Shylock weder als Witzfigur noch als Bösewicht", erläuterte Pacino seine Interpretation der Figur. „In meinen Augen ist er ein Mensch, der sich gegen das System stellt." / « Je ne vois pas Shylock comme un personnage comique ou détestable », déclare Al Pacino. « Pour moi, c'est un homme aux prises avec le système. »

STILL FROM 'ANGELS IN AMERICA' (2003)
Pacino, under the direction of Mike Nichols, haunted on his deathbed by Meryl Streep (right) as his mother's ghost. / Unter der Regie von Mike Nichols wird Cohn auf seinem Sterbebett vom Geist seiner Mutter heimgesucht, gespielt von Meryl Streep (rechts). / Filmé par Mike Nichols sur son lit de mort, Roy Cohn est hanté par le fantôme de sa mère (Meryl Streep).

STILL FROM 'TWO FOR THE MONEY' (2005)
Matthew McConaughey (right) is a professional athlete,
sidelined by an injury, in a Faustian bargain with Pacino's
top gambling tout. / Matthew McConaughey (rechts) ist
ein Profisportler, den eine Verletzung außer Gefecht
gesetzt hat und der einen Faust'schen Pakt mit Walter
Abrams (Pacino) schließt, der Tipps für hohe
Sportwetten verkauft. / Athlète professionnel mis sur
la touche par une blessure, Matthew McConaughey
(à droite) conclut un pacte diabolique avec le patron
d'une agence de paris sportifs (Pacino).

**PORTRAIT FOR
'TWO FOR THE MONEY' (2005)**
Vintage Pacino—still a leading man, but content to
dominate from the sidelines if need be. / Ein klassischer
Pacino - immer noch in der Hauptrolle, doch wenn
nötig, beherrscht er das Spiel auch von der Seitenlinie
aus. / Même s'il tient toujours la vedette, l'inoxydable
Al Pacino se contente parfois de régner en coulisses.

172

STILL FROM '88 MINUTES' (2006)
Someone has given him 88 minutes to live—but who?
Here he is entangled with his assistant (Kim Cummings,
right). / Er hat noch 88 Minuten zu leben – doch wer ist
sein Mörder? Hier greift er nach seiner Assistentin
(Kim Cummings, rechts). / Jack Gramm, qui agrippe ici
son assistante (Kim Cummings), n'a plus que 88 minutes
à vivre. Mais qui veut sa peau ?

STILL FROM '88 MINUTES' (2006)
At the center of a film that plays out in real time, as a
psychiatrist suffering the revenge of a serial killer he
sent to death row. / Im Mittelpunkt dieses Films, der in
Echtzeit spielt, steht ein Psychiater, an dem sich ein
Serienmörder rächt, der seinetwegen in der Todeszelle
landete. / Au centre de cette intrigue filmée en temps
réel, un psychiatre en proie à la vengeance du tueur en
série qu'il a expédié dans le couloir de la mort.

STILL FROM 'OCEAN'S 13' (2007)
George Clooney (left). The pleasure of these *Ocean's* films is that everyone we see is clever, dangerous, and never too serious. / Mit George Clooney (links). Die Vergnüglichkeit der Ocean's-Filme rührt daher, dass alle Figuren, die darin auftreten, clever, gefährlich und nie zu ernsthaft sind. / Avec George Clooney (à gauche). Le charme de la série des Ocean's réside dans un mélange d'intelligence, de suspense et d'humour.

STILL FROM 'OCEAN'S 13' (2007)
Here, as a menacing casino owner, Pacino creates a lightweight variant of his iconic roles—in keeping with the lightness of the film. / Als bedrohlicher Kasinobesitzer spielt Pacino eine leichtgewichtige Variante seiner Kultrollen - passend zum Humor des Films. / Pour cette comédie légère, Al Pacino concocte une version allégée de ses rôles emblématiques en campant un intraitable propriétaire de casino.

STILL FROM 'RIGHTEOUS KILL' (2008)
Pacino reunited with Robert De Niro, as New York
cops—a pair of longtime partners accustomed to
bending the rules in the law's favor. / Pacino und Robert
De Niro stehen diesmal auf der gleichen Seite des
Gesetzes als zwei New Yorker Polizisten, die schon so
lange Partner sind, dass sie sich daran gewöhnt haben,
die Regeln im Interesse des Gesetzes notfalls auch ein
wenig zu verbiegen. / Al Pacino et Robert De Niro se
retrouvent dans des rôles de vieux policiers new-
yorkais habitués à contourner le règlement pour faire
respecter la loi.

"Life is on the wire—the rest is just waiting."
Al Pacino

*„Das Leben findet auf dem Drahtseil statt – der Rest
ist nur Warterei."*
Al Pacino

*« La vie, c'est quand on est sur le fil. Le reste du
temps, on se contente d'attendre. »*
Al Pacino

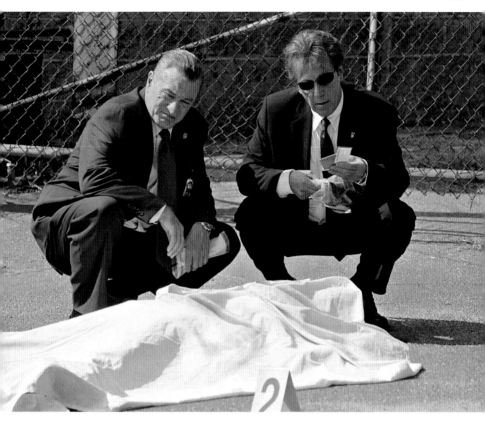

STILL FROM 'RIGHTEOUS KILL' (2008)
A serial killer, or maybe a cop, is killing criminals who
were never convicted. When they catch him, do Turk
(De Niro) and Rooster (Pacino) put the killer in jail,
or pin a medal on him? / Ein Serienmörder –
möglicherweise auch ein Polizist – tötet Verbrecher,
die nie verurteilt wurden. Werden Turk (De Niro) und
Rooster (Pacino) den Killer hinter Gitter bringen,
wenn sie ihn erwischen, oder werden sie ihm einen
Orden verleihen? / Un tueur en série s'attaque aux
criminels passés à travers les mailles du filet. Est-ce un
truand ou un policier ? Mérite-t-il la prison ou une
médaille ? Des questions que se posent Turk (De Niro)
et Rooster (Pacino).

3
CHRONOLOGY

CHRONOLOGIE
CHRONOLOGIE

CHRONOLOGY

25 April 1940 Born Alfredo Pacino, New York City. Sicilian ancestry. Father leaves family when Pacino is two years old. Raised thereafter in South Bronx by mother and grandparents.

1954 Enters Manhattan's high school for the performing arts.

1956 Drops out of school, works many menial jobs—delivery boy, usher, porter, apartment-building superintendent. Longest-held job is as an office boy for *Commentary* magazine, where he makes the acquaintances of editor Norman Podhoretz and writer Susan Sontag.

1959 After saving enough money, attends Herbert Berghof's acting school.

1962 Death of his mother, Rose. "I went to pieces." Pacino, 22, suffers insomnia, risks a mental breakdown. A nurse offers to have him committed. Shocked, he pulls himself together.

1966 Enters Lee Strasberg's Actors Studio.

1967 While performing in Boston, Pacino meets and falls in love with actress Jill Clayburgh. Their passionate relationship is the first of many between Pacino and various actresses, among them Tuesday Weld, Marthe Keller, Kathleen Quinlan, Diane Keaton, Jan Tarrant, and Beverly D'Angelo.

1968 Wins Obie ["off-Broadway"] Award for his performance as a psychotic urban bully in *The Indian Wants the Bronx*, written by Israel Horovitz.

1969 Wins Tony Award for his Broadway debut as a drug addict in *Does a Tiger Wear a Necktie?* Makes film debut in *Me, Natalie*.

1971 Oustanding performance in *The Panic in Needle Park* wins the admiration of film director Francis Ford Coppola, who casts Pacino as Michael Corleone in *The Godfather* (1972).

1972 Nominated for the Academy Award for best supporting actor for *The Godfather*.

1974 Nominated for the Academy Award for best actor for *The Godfather: Part II*.

1977 Returns to Broadway in *The Basic Training of Pavlo Hummel* by David Rabe. Wins second Tony Award.

1982–1984 Serves as co-artistic director, with Ellen Burstyn, of the Actors Studio.

1990 Birth of daughter, Julie Marie. Her mother is Jan Tarrant, a former acting teacher at the Strasberg Institute.

1992 After being nominated for Oscars for *Serpico, Dog Day Afternoon, … And Justice for All*, and *Glengarry Glen Ross*, Pacino wins the Academy Award for best actor for his performance in *Scent of a Woman*.

2001 Birth of twins, Anton and Olivia. Their mother is actress Beverly D'Angelo.

2006 *Al Pacino: An Actor's Vision* is released. It is a four-DVD box set comprising his efforts as a director and producer, including *The Local Stigmatic*, *Chinese Coffee*, and bonus material.

ON THE SET OF 'THE GODFATHER' (1972)

CHRONOLOGIE

25. April 1940 Er kommt als Alfredo Pacino in New York City zur Welt. Seine Familie stammt aus Sizilien. Der Vater lässt sie sitzen, als Al zwei Jahre alt ist. Danach wächst er in der Süd-Bronx bei seiner Mutter und seinen Großeltern auf.

1954 Er geht in Manhattan auf die Highschool für Darstellende Künste.

1956 Er verlässt die Schule und nimmt zahlreiche Jobs für ungelernte Kräfte an: Laufbursche, Platzanweiser, Kofferträger, Hausmeister in einer Wohnanlage. Am längsten arbeitet er als Bürojunge für die jüdische Zeitschrift *Commentary*, wo er Chefredakteur Norman Podhoretz und die Schriftstellerin Susan Sontag kennenlernt.

1959 Nachdem er genügend Geld angespart hat, besucht er Herbert Berghofs Schauspielschule.

1962 Seine Mutter Rose stirbt. „Ich war am Boden zerstört." Pacino (22) leidet unter Schlaflosigkeit und steht kurz vor einem Nervenzusammenbruch. Eine Krankenschwester schlägt die Einweisung in eine Anstalt vor, woraufhin er sich schockiert zusammenreißt.

1966 Er nimmt Schauspielunterricht im Actors Studio von Lee Strasberg.

1967 Während einer Vorstellung in Boston lernt Pacino seine Kollegin Jill Clayburgh kennen und verliebt sich in sie. Ihre leidenschaftliche Beziehung ist die erste von vielen zwischen Pacino und diversen Schauspielerinnen, darunter Tuesday Weld, Marthe Keller, Kathleen Quinlan, Diane Keaton, Jan Tarrant und Beverly D'Angelo.

1968 Er erhält einen "Obie ['Off-Broadway'] Award" für seine Darstellung eines psychotischen Stadttyrannen in *The Indian Wants the Bronx*, einem Theaterstück von Israel Horovitz.

**PORTRAIT FOR
'FRANKIE AND JOHNNY' (1991)**

1969 Er wird mit einem "Tony Award" für sein Broadway-Debüt als Drogenabhängiger in *Does a Tiger Wear a Necktie?* ausgezeichnet. Er gibt sein Filmdebüt in *Ich, Natalie*.

1971 Francis Ford Coppola bewundert seine herausragende darstellerische Leistung in dem Film *The Panic in Needle Park* und gibt ihm daraufhin die Rolle des Michael Corleone in *Der Pate* (1972).

1972 Er wird für seine Rolle in *Der Pate* für einen Oscar als bester Nebendarsteller nominiert.

1974 Er wird für die gleiche Rolle in *Der Pate: Teil 2* für einen Oscar als bester Hauptdarsteller nominiert.

1977 Er kehrt in David Rabes Stück *The Basic Training of Pavlo Hummel* an den Broadway zurück und gewinnt seinen zweiten "Tony Award".

1982–1984 Mit Ellen Burstyn zusammen übernimmt er die künstlerische Leitung des Actors Studio.

1990 Seine Tochter Julie Marie kommt zur Welt. Ihre Mutter ist Jan Tarrant, eine ehemalige Schauspiellehrerin am Strasberg-Institut.

1992 Nachdem er für seine Rollen in *Serpico, Hundstage, ... und Gerechtigkeit für alle* und *Glengarry Glen Ross* für Oscars nominiert worden war, erhält Pacino endlich die begehrte Trophäe als bester Hauptdarsteller für seine Rolle in *Der Duft der Frauen*.

2001 Geburt der Zwillinge Anton James und Olivia Rose, deren Mutter die Schauspielerin Beverly D'Angelo ist.

2006 *Al Pacino: An Actor's Vision*, eine Box mit vier DVDs, kommt in den Handel. Sie enthält neben Bonusmaterial Pacinos Werke als Regisseur und Produzent – darunter *The Local Stigmatic* und *Chinese Coffee*.

CHRONOLOGIE

25 avril 1940 Naissance à New York d'Alfredo Pacino, issu d'une famille sicilienne. Son père quitte le foyer quand il a deux ans. Il est élevé dans le Bronx par sa mère et ses grands-parents.

1954 Entre à la High School of Performing Arts de New York.

1956 Quitte l'école et vit de petits boulots (livreur, ouvreur, portier, concierge). Travaille comme garçon de bureau au magazine *Commentary*, où il rencontre le rédacteur en chef Norman Podhoretz et l'écrivain Susan Sontag.

1959 Après avoir économisé suffisamment d'argent, étudie à l'école d'art dramatique d'Herbert Berghof.

1962 Âgé de 22 ans à la mort de sa mère Rose, Al Pacino souffre d'insomnie et frôle la dépression nerveuse. Choqué qu'une infirmière ait proposé de l'interner, il parvient à se ressaisir.

1966 Entre à l'Actors Studio de Lee Strasberg.

1967 Lors d'une représentation à Boston, Al Pacino rencontre l'actrice Jill Clayburgh, dont il tombe amoureux. Leur relation passionnée est la première d'une longue série de liaisons avec des actrices, parmi lesquelles Tuesday Weld, Marthe Keller, Kathleen Quinlan, Diane Keaton, Jan Tarrant et Beverly D'Angelo.

1968 Remporte un «Obie» (Off-Broadway Theater Award) pour son rôle de caïd psychotique dans la pièce *L'Indien cherche le Bronx* d'Israel Horovitz.

1969 Remporte un Tony Award pour ses débuts à Broadway dans un rôle de toxicomane dans *Does a Tiger Wear a Necktie?* Fait ses débuts au cinéma dans *Me, Natalie*.

1971 Sa remarquable interprétation dans *Panique à Needle Park* lui vaut l'admiration du réalisateur Francis Ford Coppola, qui lui confie le rôle de Michael Corleone dans *Le Parrain* (1972).

1972 Sélectionné pour l'oscar du Meilleur second rôle dans *Le Parrain*.

1974 Sélectionné pour l'oscar du Meilleur acteur dans *Le Parrain, 2ᵉ partie*.

1977 Retourne à Broadway dans *The Basic Training of Pavlo Hummel* de David Rabe, qui lui vaut un second Tony Award.

1982–1984 Devient codirecteur artistique de l'Actors Studio avec Ellen Burstyn.

1990 Naissance de sa fille Julie Marie, dont la mère est Jan Tarrant, ancien professeur au Lee Strasberg Institute.

1992 Après avoir été sélectionné aux Oscars pour *Serpico*, *Un après-midi de chien*, *Justice pour tous* et *Glengarry*, il remporte celui du meilleur acteur pour *Le Temps d'un week-end*.

2001 Naissance de ses jumeaux Anton et Olivia, dont la mère est l'actrice Beverly D'Angelo.

2006 Sortie de *Al Pacino: An Actor's Vision*, coffret de quatre DVD contenant les films qu'il a réalisés et produits (notamment *The Local Stigmatic* et *Chinese Coffee*), ainsi que des bonus.

ON THE SET OF 'THE GODFATHER' (1972)

FRANCIS FORD COPPOLA'S

The Godfather
PART III

4
FILMOGRAPHY

FILMOGRAFIE
FILMOGRAPHIE

Me, Natalie (dt. *Ich, Natalie*, 1969)
Tony. Director/Regie/réalisation: Fred Coe.

The Panic in Needle Park (fr. *Panique à Needle Park*, 1971)
Bobby. Director/Regie/réalisation: Jerry Schatzberg.

The Godfather (dt. *Der Pate*, fr. *Le Parrain*, 1972)
Michael Corleone. Director/Regie/réalisation: Francis Ford Coppola.

Scarecrow (dt. *Asphalt-Blüten*, fr. *L'Épouvantail*, 1973)
Francis Lionel "Lion" Delbuchi. Director/Regie/réalisation: Jerry Schatzberg.

Serpico (1973)
Frank Serpico. Director/Regie/réalisation: Sidney Lumet.

The Godfather: Part II (dt. *Der Pate: Teil 2*, fr. *Le Parrain, 2ᵉ partie*, 1974)
Michael Corleone. Director/Regie/réalisation: Francis Ford Coppola.

Dog Day Afternoon (dt. *Hundstage*, fr. *Un après-midi de chien*, 1975)
Sonny Wortzik. Director/Regie/réalisation: Sidney Lumet.

Bobby Deerfield (1977)
Bobby Deerfield. Director/Regie/réalisation: Sydney Pollack.

... And Justice for All (dt. *... und Gerechtigkeit für alle*, fr. *Justice pour tous*, 1979)
Arthur Kirkland. Director/Regie/réalisation: Norman Jewison.

Cruising (fr. *La Chasse*, 1980)
Steve Burns. Director/Regie/réalisation: William Friedkin.

Author! Author! (dt. *Daddy! Daddy! Fünf Nervensägen und ein Vater*, fr. *Avec les compliments de l'auteur*, 1982)
Ivan Travalian. Director/Regie/réalisation: Arthur Hiller.

Scarface (1983)
Tony Montana. Director/Regie/réalisation: Brian De Palma.

Revolution (fr. *Révolution*, 1985)
Tom Dobb. Director/Regie/réalisation: Hugh Hudson.

The Local Stigmatic (filmed in 1986/gedreht 1986/tourné en 1986)
Graham. Director/Regie/réalisation: Al Pacino.

Sea of Love (dt. *Melodie des Todes*, fr. *Mélodie pour un meurtre*, 1989)
Detective Frank Keller. Director/Regie/réalisation: Harold Becker.

Dick Tracy (1990)
Big Boy Caprice. Director/Regie/réalisation: Warren Beatty.

The Godfather: Part III (dt. *Der Pate: Teil 3*, fr. *Le Parrain, 3ᵉ partie*, 1990)
Michael Corleone. Director/Regie/réalisation: Francis Ford Coppola.

Frankie and Johnny (dt. *Frankie und Johnny*, fr. *Frankie & Johnny*, 1991)
Johnny. Director/Regie/réalisation: Garry Marshall.

Glengarry Glen Ross (fr. *Glengarry*, 1992)
Ricky Roma. Director/Regie/réalisation: James Foley.

Scent of a Woman (dt. *Der Duft der Frauen*, fr. *Le Temps d'un week-end*, 1992)
Lieutenant Colonel Frank Slade. Director/Regie/réalisation: Martin Brest.

Carlito's Way (fr. *L'Impasse*, 1993)
Carlito "Charlie" Brigante. Director/Regie/réalisation: Brian De Palma.

Two Bits (dt. *25 Cents: Höre nie auf, dir etwas zu wünschen*, fr. *Instant de bonheur*, 1995)
Gitano Sabatoni. Director/Regie/réalisation: James Foley.

Heat (1995)
Lieutenant Vincent Hanna. Director/Regie/réalisation: Michael Mann.

City Hall (1995)
Mayor/Bürgermeister/le maire John Pappas. Director/Regie/réalisation: Harold Becker.

Looking for Richard (dt. *Al Pacino's Looking for Richard*, 1996)
Himself/Richard III//Al Pacino/Richard III. Director/Regie/réalisation: Al Pacino.

Donnie Brasco (1997)
Benjamin "Lefty" Ruggiero. Director/Regie/réalisation: Mike Newell.

The Devil's Advocate (dt. *Im Auftrag des Teufels*, fr. *L'Associé du diable*, 1997)
John Milton (Satan). Director/Regie/réalisation: Taylor Hackford.

The Insider (dt. aka *Insider*, fr. *Révélations*, 1999)
Lowell Bergman. Director/Regie/réalisation: Michael Mann.

Any Given Sunday (dt. *An jedem verdammten Sonntag*, fr. *L'Enfer du dimanche*, 1999)
Coach Tony D'Amato. Director/Regie/réalisation: Oliver Stone.

Chinese Coffee (2000)
Harry Levine. Director/Regie/réalisation: Al Pacino.

S1m0ne (2002)
Viktor Taransky. Director/Regie/réalisation: Andrew Niccol.

Insomnia (dt. *Schlaflos*, 2002)
Detective Will Dormer. Director/Regie/réalisation: Christopher Nolan.

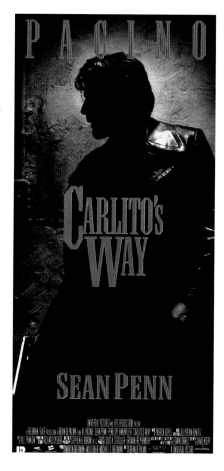

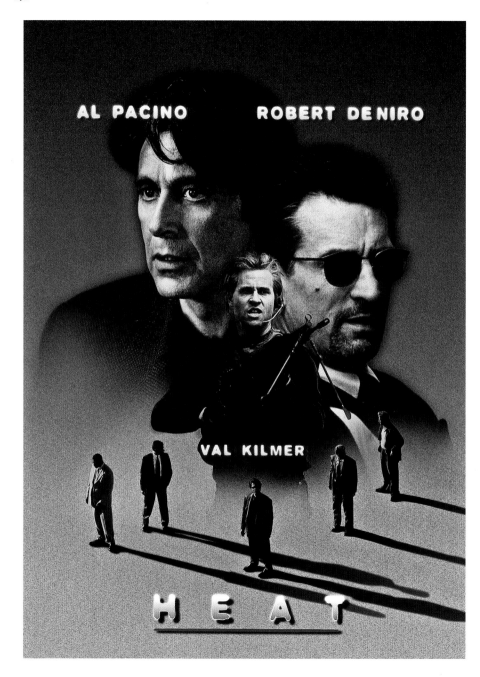

Gigli (dt. *Liebe mit Risiko*, fr. *Amours troubles*, 2003)
Starkman. Director/Regie/réalisation: Martin Brest.

People I Know (dt. *Im inneren Kreis*, fr. *Influences*, 2003)
Eli Wurman. Director/Regie/réalisation: Daniel Algrant.

The Recruit (dt. *Der Einsatz*, fr. *La Recrue*, 2003)
Walter Burke. Director/Regie/réalisation: Roger Donaldson.

Angels in America (dt. *Engel in Amerika*, 2003)
Roy Cohn. Director/Regie/réalisation: Mike Nichols.

The Merchant of Venice (dt. *Der Kaufmann von Venedig*, 2004)
Shylock. Director/Regie/réalisation: Michael Radford.

Two for the Money (dt. *Das schnelle Geld*, 2005)
Walter Abrams. Director/Regie/réalisation: D. J. Caruso.

88 Minutes (2006)
Dr. Jack Gramm. Director/Regie/réalisation: Jon Avnet.

Ocean's 13 (2007)
Willy Bank. Director/Regie/réalisation: Steven Soderbergh.

Righteous Kill (dt. *Kurzer Prozess*, fr. *La Loi et l'Ordre*, 2008)
Rooster. Director/Regie/réalisation: Jon Avnet.

Salomaybe? (2009)
Himself/King Herod//Al Pacino/König Herodes// Al Pacino/roi Hérode. Director/Regie/réalisation: Al Pacino.

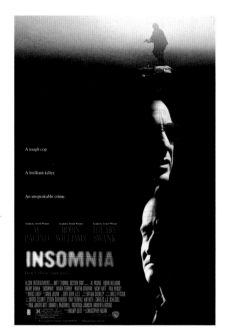

BIBLIOGRAPHY

Cieutat (Michel) & Viviani (Christian): *Al Pacino, Robert de Niro. Regards croisés.* Paris, 2000.
Grobel, Lawrence: *Al Pacino: The Authorized Biography.* New York, 2007.
Schoell, William: *The Films of Al Pacino.* New York, 1995.
Yule, Andrew: *Life on the Wire: The Life and Art of Al Pacino.* New York, 1991.

IMPRINT

© 2009 TASCHEN GmbH
Hohenzollernring 53, D-50672 Köln
www.taschen.com

Editor/Picture Research: Paul Duncan/Wordsmith Solutions
Editorial Coordination: Martin Holz, Cologne
Production Coordination: Nadia Najm and Horst Neuzner, Cologne
German Translation: Thomas J. Kinne, Nauheim
French Translation: Anne Le Bot, Paris
Multilingual Production: www.arnaudbriand.com, Paris
Typeface Design: Sense/Net, Andy Disl and Birgit Eichwede, Cologne

Printed in China
ISBN 978-3-8365-0856-8

To stay informed about upcoming TASCHEN titles, please request our magazine at www.taschen.com/magazine or write to TASCHEN, Hohenzollernring 53, D-50672 Cologne, Germany, contact@taschen.com, Fax: +49-221-254919. We will be happy to send you a free copy of our magazine which is filled with information about all of our books.

SEP 1 5 2009